MINNESOTA JOB SEEKER'S SOURCEBOOK

"#1 RESOURCE GUIDE I'd use for a first-rate Minnesota job search."

— **Joyce Lain Kennedy**

Author, Hook Up. Get Hired! *and* The Electronic Resume Revolution
Nationally Syndicated Career Columnist, Los Angeles Times Syndicate

---

"REQUIRED READING! Nothing compares with the detail and accuracy of the *Minnesota Job Seeker's Sourcebook*. The time and energy saved by using this guide makes it an essential tool for job seekers. Buy it and use it!"

Kevin Nutter, Ph.D., Director, Career Development Center, University of Minnesota

---

"BEST JOB SEARCH BOOK for useful information and sensible advice."

Mark Gisleson, Founder, Minnesota Resume Network

"GOLD MINE! Complete and thorough, the one-stop job-help sourcebook."

Colleen Watson, MA, CPC, Past President, Minnesota Asso. of Personnel Services

---

"TOP-DRAWER REFERRAL TOOL for job seekers and the people who help them. Don't be surprised if you wear out your copy!"

Sandy Kuntz, Producer and Host, "Career Conversations" Cable Broadcast

---

"POWER-PACKED ROAD MAP for anyone navigating from yesterday's pink slip to tomorrow's new job."

Paula Ancona, Author
SuccessAbilities! 1001 Practical Ways to Keep Up, Stand Out & Move Ahead at Work

---

"QUICK LINK to the career experts that job seekers need to succeed."

Rich Murray, President, Minnesota College and University Placement Association
Director, St. Cloud State University Career Services

IT'S A WINNER!

Minnesota Job Seeker's Sourcebook

"BEST INFORMATION GUIDE"
1995 MINNESOTA BOOK AWARD

"BEST CONSUMER DIRECTORY"
NATIONAL DIRECTORY PUBLISHING ASSOCIATION
1995 SILVER MEDAL

"BEST BOOK ABOUT THE MIDWEST"
1995 MIDWEST BOOK ACHIEVEMENT AWARD

"BEST PAGE DESIGN"
NATIONAL DIRECTORY PUBLISHING ASSOCIATION
1995 GOLD MEDAL

"BEST LISTING READABILITY"
NATIONAL DIRECTORY PUBLISHING ASSOCIATION
1995 GOLD MEDAL

"BEST PRINT QUALITY"
NATIONAL DIRECTORY PUBLISHING ASSOCIATION
1995 GOLD MEDAL

"BEST USE OF TYPOGRAPHY"
NATIONAL DIRECTORY PUBLISHING ASSOCIATION
1995 GOLD MEDAL

"BEST ALL-AROUND BOOK"
1992 MINNESOTA BOOK ACHIEVEMENT MERIT AWARD

MINNESOTA

JOB SEEKER'S

SOURCEBOOK

THE COMPLETE STATEWIDE GUIDE TO JOB-SEEKING SUPPORT SERVICES

Edited by Pati Gelfman

THIRD EDITION

RESOURCE PUBLISHING GROUP, INC.

Minnetonka, Minnesota

Minnesota Job Seeker's Sourcebook
The Complete Guide To Minnesota Job Seeking Support Services

Third Edition, First Printing   1996

PRINTED IN THE UNITED STATES OF AMERICA

ISBN 0-9629615-2-3

Resource Publishing Group, Inc.
P.O. Box 573
Hopkins, Minnesota 55343 USA

Cover design: Jonathan Gelfman

This book is dedicated to
My loving husband, Buddy, and children
Anna, Jesse, Michael, Jon, Amy, Judy and Dan
A bright and happy clan
Generous and hard-working
Who rise above life's inevitable obstacles
To live life to its fullest
Who constantly inspire me
And remind me
That dreams
Are meant to be reached.

PSG

Other career resources available from

RESOURCE PUBLISHING GROUP INC.

NEW! MINNESOTA CAREER STORE

http://www.careerstore.com

The all-new Minnesota Career Store is your online gateway to a sampler edition of the Twin Cities Job Seeker's Calendar, unique career resources, best tips for Minnesota job seekers and links to useful Internet employment sites. Available spring 1996.

QUICKSTART TOOL KITS

Our most popular collection of powerhouse job-search tools! For job seekers, recent graduates, dislocated workers, alumni groups and corporate outplacement support. Call for details.

JOB SEEKER'S ACTION PLANNER

Get yourself or your clients organized with this combination daily/weekly planner and goal-setting tool. 40-page tablet. Available in tool kits above or in quantities to organizations.

TWIN CITIES JOB SEEKER'S CALENDAR

Monthly calendar of Twin Cities job-seeking events. Available to libraries, schools and career services by annual subscription.

JOB SEARCH RESOURCE SERIES

Practical and powerful outplacement resource series for displaced employees. Minnesota and national editions.

Call about these and other workplace products and services from

RESOURCE PUBLISHING GROUP
P.O. BOX 573 HOPKINS, MN 55343

TWIN CITIES **(612) 545-5980**   **(800) 555-9058**

WITH SPECIAL
THANKS

This completely revised third edition of the *Minnesota Job Seeker's Sourcebook*—with a crisp new look, new chapters and over 1,000 job-search resources—is a testament to the hard work, insight, creativity and skills of many people. Special thanks to these individuals:

RESEARCH AND DESIGN TEAM: Pati Gelfman, Tami Ruden, Donna Wallace, Anna Simon, Donna Campbell, Jonathan and Amy Gelfman.

SPECIAL CONTRIBUTORS: Colleen Watson, Sandy Kuntz, Beverly Kontola, Heidi Stennes, Diane Tessari, Paula Ancona, Leo Bright, Caron Hassen and Joyce Lain Kennedy.

COMMUNITY ADVISORS: Debbie Atterberry, Vicky Bacal, Shirley Baker, Sue Banovetz, Christine Chelstrom, Elizabeth Craig, Joe Crowe, John Eckberg, Pat Foulkes, Kathleen Franey, Pat Gallatin, Jeanne Gehrman, Mark Gisleson, Larry Greenbaum, Nedra Halsted, Sinead Higgins, Rise Kasmirski, Stephen Koller, Mark Larson, Donna Leviton, Amy Lindgren, Rick Matson, Rich Murray, Lynn Miller, Kevin Nutter, Yvette Oldendorf, Joe Oliver, Gerry Nelson, Eric Radtke, Julie Remington, Brent Rothgeb, Bob Rystrom, Donald Sayner, Mary Sickel, Daniel Swalm, Lonna Szczesny, Chip Wells, Wayne Young, Terry Zurn.

FAMILY AND FRIENDS: Mark Gelfman, Anna Simon, Jesse Simon, Jonathan and Amy Gelfman, Mike, Judy and Dan Gelfman, Allison Schultz, Stacy Kaplan, David Briefstein, Dorothy and Ted Papermaster, Ruth Gelfman, Stuart Marrs, the Tatarka family, Barb Clayman, Rhoda Levin, Gail and Al Bender, Jill Marks and Chuck Cook.

TABLE OF
CONTENTS

INTRODUCTION

＊＊＊＊＊

By virtue of picking up this book, chances are good you are:

◆ Recently out of a job;

◆ Exploring a new career direction or job change;

◆ Seriously entering the job market for the first time;

◆ Re-entering the job market after a long absence; or

◆ Planning a job move to, or within Minnesota

Your first assignment is to get organized. Today, a productive job hunt begins by aligning the resources you need to proceed with competence and confidence. But figuring out *where* to find guidance or support can take almost as much time and energy as finding a job.

The *Minnesota Job Seeker's Sourcebook* makes quick work of linking you to the job-help resources you need to succeed. We've done the homework so you can concentrate on your #1 task—landing your next position.

The *Minnesota Job Seeker's Sourcebook* includes over 1,000 up-to-date resources located throughout Minnesota and nationwide. With the help of this award-winning one-stop guide, you can confidently move forward to: 1) focus your job hunt, (2) track down job leads, (3) tap support networks, (4) link to online and multimedia job-seeking resources, and (5) explore worklife alternatives.

If you are a busy career or employment professional, the *Minnesota Job Seeker's Sourcebook* is a first-rate referral tool. Use it as a daily reference guide for yourself and as a resource in your client library.

To our knowledge, no other directory in the nation compares with the *Minnesota Job Seeker's Sourcebook*. No other state guide offers job seekers such an extensive variety of local resources. No other Minnesota job-help guide has elicited such praise or earned such popularity.

In this new edition we have worked hard to maintain your trust in our thorough research and our pulse on the trends.

Here's what's new in this revised third edition:

- ◆ COMPLETELY UPDATED information; hundreds of NEW listings
- ◆ NEW CHAPTER: Online & Multimedia Job-Search Resources
- ◆ RE-DESIGNED easy-reading format
- ◆ E-MAIL AND INTERNET addresses added to many listings
- ◆ EASY-TO-FOLLOW geographic distinctions between Twin Cities and Greater Minnesota resources
- ◆ EXPANDED sections on Job Hotlines, Search Firms, Hot Tips
- ◆ LATE-BREAKING information about the new Minnesota Workforce Centers.

We hope that this book leads you to those who offer you advice or solutions which, in turn, lead you to your dream job.

To your success!

Pati Gelfman
Publisher

HOW TO USE
THIS BOOK

The *Minnesota Job Seeker's Sourcebook* is designed to be a user-friendly clearinghouse of job-seeking resources.

Here are some tips on how to use this guide

◆ The book is organized into six chapters that address basic job-seeking needs. For your convenience, chapters can be accessed in random order.

◆ Resources are grouped into two geographic regions: (1) Twin Cities metro area and (2) Greater Minnesota. An easy-to-read header at the top of each page designates the region represented below it. As you will note, several sections have no regional headers. These sections predominantly include products or services that have statewide appeal.

◆ Listings generally include the name of the organization or product, address, local phone number, 800 number, fax number, Internet address and E-mail address. The description briefly explains what services or features to expect, who is eligible, how to apply or purchase and basic pricing information.

◆ Several regions in Minnesota have been affected by area code changes. Listings in this edition reflect the most up-to-date information including the state's new "320" area code.

◆ Every chapter and sub-chapter is preceded by a short article that offers tips and suggestions about what services or features to expect, what questions to ask and, in some cases, what to watch out for.

◆ **It's up to you to be a smart consumer of job-help services.**
Before paying fees, understand what you will get for your money and
how you will benefit from the products or services. Interview the
prospective service thoroughly. Ask for references. Clarify charges. Not
every organization has your best interests at heart. Don't waste
precious money, time, energy or patience on a service that will not
perform to your expectations.

◆ **How to resolve a problem with an organization:** If you have
been unsuccessful in resolving a problem directly with an organization,
here are some steps to consider. Contact your local consumer
protection office, Better Business Bureau, the appropriate state
licensing board, professional association or the Minnesota Attorney
General's Office, (612) 296-6196 or (800) 657-3787.

◆ **Help us stay on top of change!** Please keep us informed if you
encounter listing information that's no longer current. We make
every effort to keep our database up to date between publishing
dates and your feedback is welcome! Please contact Resource
Publishing Group, P.O. Box 573, Hopkins, MN, 55343. Phone—(612)
545-5980   Fax—(612) 545-9241   E-mail—RPG@primenet.com

◆ **Free updates & additions:** Did you borrow this book? If you're
planning to purchase this edition of the *Minnesota Job Seeker's
Sourcebook*—and you purchase it directly from Resource Publishing
Group—you will also receive a free copy of "Late-Breaking Updates and
Additions" with any book order placed after October, 1996. An Order
Form can be found on page 288.

CHAPTER ONE

FOR
JOB SEARCH
GUIDANCE

- State Government Job Centers
- Career Coaching Services
  Non-Profit & Local Government
- Career Coaching Services
  Private Sector
- Resume Specialists
- School-based Career Centers

L ooking for a job, choosing a new career path or seriously entering the job market for the first time is downright hard work. At times it can be frustrating. At other times insightful. For those who lose their jobs suddenly, or at an advanced age, the loss can be a major blow.

If you are plunging into the job market, slow down and focus your efforts. Understand your strengths and skills. Set goals. Map out a strategy. Align your resources before you push ahead looking for a job. The more you understand about who you are and what you have to offer an employer, the less time you'll spend in your search.

This chapter is your primary road map to the many local people and places that can help you chart your work transition and stay on track. Some services listed in this section can help you explore your skills, interests and career goals. Others can help you master specific techniques of the job search. Still others offer access to state-of-the-art career resource centers. Some full-service organizations do it all.

STATE GOVERNMENT
JOB CENTERS

If you equate state-run job centers with dingy grey walls and charity handouts, perish the thought. While it's true these offices are not likely homes to mahogany conference tables or wild life art, don't second-guess the value of their services.

Even if you've never before turned to the state for job help—for reemployment insurance, job-search coaching, employment leads—explore your options with an open mind.

At the time of this writing, Congress is expected to pass new legislation eliminating dozens of complicated federal jobs programs. In their places, each state may receive sizable sums of money to design and run more flexible, user-friendly services.

Minnesota is already emerging as one of the nation's visionary leaders. The state's new initiative—the **Minnesota Workforce Center**—is a network of one-stop centers where job seekers can tap a variety of free employment services. These services range from high-tech job matching systems to people-focused personal guidance. And more. See page 22 for details.

This symbol ▲ found throughout this and the following section, identifies organizations linked to a growing network of employment, training and human services coordinated with the Minnesota Workforce Centers. These community partners are working together to make access to a broad range of job transition services quick and easy.

YOUR ROAD MAP TO STATE EMPLOYMENT SERVICES

"Where can I apply for reemployment insurance?"

- Job Service/Reemployment Insurance Offices, page 19.

"Where can I get free access to computers, telephones to use during office hours, job-search resources and workshops?"

- Job Service/Reemployment Insurance Offices, page 19.
- Minnesota Workforce Centers (if located in your area), page 22.

"How can I track down qualified job leads—even if I'm a manager or professional?"

- Job Service/Reemployment Insurance Offices, page 19.
- Minnesota Workforce Centers (if located in your area), page 22.

"Who can tell me whether I qualify for specialized services including skills retraining?"

- Job Service/Reemployment Insurance Offices, page 19.
- Minnesota Workforce Centers (if located in your area), page 22.
- Look for organizations preceded by this symbol ▲.

"If I'm a Veteran, where can I get services to meet my needs?"

- Veterans Employment Services, page 26.
- Job Service/Reemployment Insurance Offices, page 19.

"What about help for people with disabilities or who are blind?"

- Special Job Seeking Needs, page 27.
- Minnesota Workforce Centers (if located in your area), page 22.

JOB SERVICE / REEMPLOYMENT INSURANCE
Minnesota Department of Economic Security

Lost your job? The Job Service/Reemployment Insurance Office is your first place to turn for reemployment benefits and job placement. Veterans also receive special attention and services. Ask a Job Service representative about benefits and whether you qualify for special programs that offer individualized job-search coaching, tuition for retraining and other support.

Some Job Service offices provide complete resource centers. Job seekers have access to computerized labor market information, interest/aptitude testing, job clubs, job postings, job-search workshops, personal computers and telephones to use during office hours—all for free or at a nominal cost.

The Job Service recently introduced **Minnesota SkillsNet,** a high-tech computer system targeted to white-collar job seekers that scans applicants' resumes and matches them with current job openings. To participate, contact your nearest Job Service office.

TWIN CITIES LOCATIONS

▲ **BLAINE**
1201 89th Ave. N.E.
Blaine, MN 55434
(612) 785-6450

▲ **MINNEAPOLIS**
1200 Plymouth Ave. No.
Minneapolis, MN 55411
(612) 520-3500

MINNEAPOLIS
777 E. Lake Street
Minneapolis, MN 55407
(612) 821-4000

▲ **MINNETONKA**
6121 Baker Road
Minnetonka, MN 55345
(612) 945-3600

▲ **NORTH ST. PAUL**
2098 E. 11th Ave.
No. St. Paul, MN 55109
(612) 779-5666

▲ **SHAKOPEE**
1136A Shakopee Town Square
Shakopee, MN 55379
(612) 496-4160

▲ **ST. PAUL**
2455 University Ave. W.
St. Paul, MN 55114
(612) 642-0363

▲ **STILLWATER**
14900 61st St. No.
Stillwater, MN 55082
(612) 297-2440

▲ **WEST ST. PAUL**
60 E. Marie
W. St. Paul, MN 55118
(612) 552-5000

JOB SERVICE / REEMPLOYMENT INSURANCE
Minnesota Department of Economic Security

GREATER MINNESOTA LOCATIONS

▲ **ALBERT LEA**
1649 W. Main Street
Albert Lea, MN 56007
(507) 373-3951

ALEXANDRIA
418 Third Ave. East
Alexandria, MN 56308
(320) 762-7800

AUSTIN
1900 8th Ave. N.W.
Austin, MN 55912
(507) 433-0555

BEMIDJI
1819 Bemidji Ave.
Bemidji, MN 56601
(218) 755-2936

▲ **BRAINERD**
1919 So. 6th St.
Brainerd, MN 56401
(218) 828-2450

▲ **CAMBRIDGE**
1575 E. Hwy. 95
Cambridge, MN 55008
(612) 689-7136

▲ **CROOKSTON**
721 So. Minnesota St.
Crookston, MN 56716
(218) 281-6020

▲ **DETROIT LAKES**
801 Roosevelt Ave.
Detroit Lakes, MN 56502
(218) 847-3136

DULUTH
320 W. Second Street
Duluth, MN 55802
(218) 723-4730

DULUTH
4921 Matterhorn Dr.
Duluth, MN 55811
(218) 723-4875

EAST GRAND FORKS
1616 Central Ave. N.E.
P.O. Box 666
E. Grand Forks, MN
56721
(218) 773-9841

▲ **FAIRMONT**
923 No. State Street
Fairmont, MN 56031
(507) 235-5518

FARIBAULT
Fairbo Town Square
P.O. Box 9
Faribault, MN 55021
(507) 332-3220

FERGUS FALLS
125 W. Lincoln Ave.
Fergus Falls, MN 56538
(218) 739-7560

GRAND RAPIDS
409 13th St. S.E.
Grand Rapids, MN
55744
(218) 327-4480

▲ **HIBBING**
Mesabi Mall
Hibbing, MN 55746
(218) 262-6777

▲ **HUTCHINSON**
P.O. Box 550
Hutchinson, MN 55350
(320) 587-4740

INTERNATIONAL FALLS
407 Fourth Street
International Falls, MN
56649
(218) 283-9427

LITCHFIELD
114 No. Holcombe Ave.
P.O. Box 1001
Litchfield, MN 55355
(320) 693-2859

GREATER MINNESOTA

LITTLE FALLS
211 S.E. First Street
Little Falls, MN 56345
(320) 632-5427

MANKATO
1650 Madison Ave.
Mankato, MN 56002
(507) 389-6723

▲ **MARSHALL**
1424 E. College Drive
Marshall, MN 56258
(507) 537-6236

▲ **MONTEVIDEO**
129 W. Nichols
Montevideo, MN 56265
(320) 269-8819

▲ **MOORHEAD**
715 No. 11th St.
Moorhead, MN 56560
(218) 236-2191

▲ **MORA**
130 So. Park Street
Mora, MN 55051
(320) 679-3611

▲ **NEW ULM**
1618 So. Broadway
New Ulm, MN 56073
(507) 354-3138

OWATONNA
204 E. Pearl Street
Owatonna, MN 55060
(507) 455-5850

PARK RAPIDS
1011 E. First Street
Park Rapids, MN 56470
(218) 732-3396

RED WING
1606 W. Third Street
Red Wing, MN 55066
(612) 388-3526

▲ **ROCHESTER**
300 11th Ave. N.W.
Rochester, MN 55901
(507) 285-7315

ROSEAU
205 2nd Ave. N.W.
Roseau, MN 56751
(218) 463-2233

▲ **ST. CLOUD**
3333 W. Division
St. Cloud, MN 56302
(320) 255-3266

THIEF RIVER FALLS
1301 Highway 1 East
Thief Rvr. Falls, MN 56701
(218) 681-0909

VIRGINIA
820 No. Ninth Street
Virginia, MN 55792
(218) 749-7704

▲ **WADENA**
311 Jefferson St. No.
P.O. Box 643
Wadena, MN 56482
(218) 631-3240

WASECA
105 Third Ave. N.E.
Waseca, MN 56093
(507) 835-8240

▲ **WILLMAR**
1900 Highway 294
Willmar, MN 56201
(320) 231-5174

▲ **WINONA**
52 E. Fifth Street
P.O. Box 739
Winona, MN 55987
(507) 453-2920

▲ **WORTHINGTON**
511 Tenth Street
P.O. Box 159
Worthington, MN 56187
(507) 376-3116

For an explanation of this symbol ▲ *see page 17.*

The ALL-NEW Look of Government Job Help

MINNESOTA WORKFORCE CENTERS

The Minnesota Workforce Center system is a breath of fresh air from the one-time red tape of government job programs. The goal of this path-breaking system is to create an integrated "one-stop" network of services that job seekers can tap for career information, job-search guidance, skills training and transition support. All free and open to the public.

Each local Minnesota Workforce Center is made up of several public and non-profit partners. These may include:

◆ Job Service / Reemployment Insurance Offices

◆ Local employment and training centers

◆ Community action and human services agencies

◆ Division of Rehabilitation Services

◆ State Services for the Blind

◆ Veterans Employment and Training Services

Free services, open to all job seekers, include a well-stocked resource center offering a range of self-directed tools: Computers to use to write resumes or access computerized career and labor market information. Job postings. Books, videos and other resources. Self-guided interest and aptitude tests. A bank of telephones to use to make daytime work-search calls. Job clubs and job-search workshops (possibly available at a modest fee) are also part of the typical services.

Upon registering for services or reemployment benefits, job seekers will be assessed to determine if they are eligible for specialized services.

These services may include tuition for skills retraining, personalized job-search guidance and other transition support assistance.

At the present time, this new system is only partially operational. Approximately 29 Workforce Centers are operating in Minnesota. Some are housed at one physical location. Others operate through a series of community partners from separate buildings. Services are coordinated through a centralized computer system.

▲ Minnesota Workforce Centers—Twin Cities Locations

ANOKA COUNTY
1201 89th Ave. N.E., Suite 230
Blaine, MN 55434
Information: (612) 783-4800

MINNEAPOLIS
1200 Plymouth Ave. No.
Minneapolis, MN 55411
Information: (612) 520-3500
Special Programs: (612) 529-3342

MINNETONKA
6121 Baker Road
Minnetonka, MN 55345
Information: (612) 945-3600
Employment/Training: (612) 945-3665

NORTH ST. PAUL
2098 E. 11th Ave.
North St. Paul, MN 55109
Information: (612) 779-5666

RAMSEY COUNTY
1945 Manton Street
Maplewood, MN 55109
Information: (612) 770-8900

ST. PAUL
2455 University Ave.
St. Paul, MN 55114
Information: (612) 642-0363
Employment & Training:
(612) 228-3283

SHAKOPEE
Shakopee Town Square Mall
Shakopee, MN 55379
Information: (612) 496-4160
Employment & Training:
(612) 445-7524

WASHINGTON COUNTY
14900 61st St. No.
Stillwater, MN 55082
Information: (612) 430-6850

WEST ST. PAUL
60 East Marie, Suite 209
West St. Paul, MN 55118
Information: (612) 552-5000

GREATER MINNESOTA

▲ MINNESOTA WORKFORCE CENTERS

Greater Minnesota Locations

ALBERT LEA
Skyline Mall, 1649 West Main St.
Albert Lea, MN 56007
Information: (507) 373-3951
Employment & Training:
(507) 373-4398

BRAINERD
1919 So. 6th St.
Brainerd, MN 56401
Information: (218) 828-2450
Employment/Training: (218) 829-2856

CAMBRIDGE
East Highway 95
Cambridge, MN 55008
Information: (612) 689-7136
Employment & Training:
(612) 689-9121

CROOKSTON
721 So. Minnesota
Crookston, MN 56716
Information: (218) 281-6020
Employment & Training:
(218) 281-5180

DETROIT LAKES
801 Roosevelt Ave.
Detroit Lakes, MN 56502
Information: (218) 847-3136
Employment & Training:
(218) 847-9205

DULUTH
332 City Hall
Duluth, MN 55802
Information: (218) 723-3419

FAIRMONT
923 No. State Street
Fairmont, MN 56031
Information: (507) 235-5518
Employment & Training:
(507) 238-1663

HIBBING
Mesabi Mall, 1101 East 37th Street
Hibbing, MN 55746
Information: (218) 262-6777
Employment & Training:
(218) 262-3412

HUTCHINSON
2 Century Ave.
Hutchinson, MN 55350
Information: (320) 587-4740
Employment & Training:
(320) 587-7661

MARSHALL
1424 East College Drive
Marshall, MN 56258
Information: (507) 537-6236
Employment & Training:
(507) 537-0548

GREATER MINNESOTA

MONTEVIDEO
129 W. Nichols
Montevideo, MN 56256
Information: (320) 269-8819
Employment & Training:
(320) 269-5561

MOORHEAD
715 No. 11th Street
Moorhead, MN 56560
Information: (218) 236-2191
Employment & Training:
(218) 233-1541

MORA
30 So. Park Street
Mora, MN 55051
Information: (320) 679-3611

NEW ULM
1618 So. Broadway
New Ulm, MN 56073
Information: (507) 354-3138
Employment & Training:
(507) 534-3766

ROCHESTER
Civic Drive Plaza
300 11th Ave. N.W.
Rochester, MN 55901
Information: (507) 281-7315
Employment & Training:
(507) 281-4670
Dislocated Workers:
(507) 287-9828
Older Worker Info: (507) 285-7315

ST. CLOUD
3333 W. Division
St. Cloud, MN 56302
Information: (320) 255-3266
Employment & Training:
(320) 656-3990

THIEF RIVER FALLS
1301 Highway 1 East
Thief River Falls, MN 56701
Information: (218) 681-0909

WILLMAR
1900 Highway 294 N.E.
Willmar, MN 56201
Information: (320) 231-5174
Employment & Training:
(320) 231-5174

WINONA
52 E. Fifth Street
Winona, MN 55987
Information: (507) 453-2920

WORTHINGTON
511 10th Street
Worthington, MN 56187
Information: (507) 376-3116
Employment & Training:
(507) 376-3113

For an explanation of this symbol ▲ *see page 17.*

VETERANS EMPLOYMENT SERVICES

Veterans, by law, are entitled to priority assistance through the Job Service. After registering at the Job Service, ask to see a veterans representative who can provide information about educational benefits, civil service preference, vocational rehabilitation, on-the-job training opportunities and referrals to allied agencies. Veterans also have reemployment rights protected by the Veterans Reemployment Rights Department. For information, contact the organizations listed below.

U.S. DEPARTMENT OF VETERANS AFFAIRS

Vocational Rehabilitation and Counseling Div. (28)
Bishop Henry Whipple Federal Building
Fort Snelling, St. Paul, MN 55111
(800) 827-1000

Open to disabled veterans who qualify for vocational rehabilitation. Career planning, assessment, testing, training, job placement, personalized counseling. Call for information. Free.

UNIFORMED SERVICES EMPLOYMENT AND REEMPLOYMENT RIGHTS

390 No. Robert Street
St. Paul, MN 55101
(612) 297-1186   Fax—(612) 282-2711

Assists military personnel in returning to their pre-military employer. Call for information. Free.

▲ VETERANS' EMPLOYMENT AND TRAINING SERVICE

390 No. Robert Street
St. Paul, MN 55101
(612) 296-3665   Fax—(612) 282-2711

Administers veterans programs at Job Service offices. Provides Disabled Veterans Outreach and Veterans Reemployment Rights programs.

SPECIAL EMPLOYMENT NEEDS

▲ DIVISION OF REHABILITATION SERVICES

Minnesota Department of Economic Security

Call for Minnesota locations.

Twin Cities Metro: (612) 296-5616
Greater Minnesota: (800) 328-9095

Works with individuals who have a disability that makes it hard to find, prepare for, or keep employment. Offers vocational assessment and testing, job placement, job coaching, job leads, training and adjustment counseling. Also specializes in rehab technology. Call for appointment. Services are free to qualified applicants.

▲ STATE SERVICES FOR THE BLIND

Minnesota Department of Economic Security

Call for Minnesota locations.

Twin Cities Metro: (612) 642-0500—Voice
                       (612) 642-0506—TTY
Greater Minnesota: (800) 652-9000—Voice/TTY

Employment assistance service. Open only to visually impaired Minnesota residents. Services include vocational assessment and testing, job placement, job-search coaching, job leads, training and adjustment counseling. Specializes in rehab technology. Call for appointment. Free.

CAREER COACHING

SERVICES

NON PROFITS & LOCAL GOVERNMENT

Finding help navigating your job transition may be easier and more affordable than you think.

Non-profit organizations and **local government agencies** offer a broad range of assistance to the unemployed and underemployed.

◆ The organizations listed on the following pages can help you polish up your job-seeking skills or explore new careers. You may also get resume assistance, tuition for retraining, job leads and other support services while you're between jobs. Most services are moderately priced or free to eligible participants.

◆ Some organizations are open to the public. Others are targeted to specific groups of individuals. As a result, to be served at these organizations, applicants must meet certain eligibility requirements. Don't hesitate to apply. Even if you think your former salary level or other criteria will disqualify you, you may be pleasantly surprised. Eligibility is based on many factors.

◆ When you see this symbol ▲ next to a listing, it's a reminder that the organization is linked to a network of employment, training and human services coordinated with the new Minnesota Workforce Center system. Together with its community partners, this organization can help you tap a variety of transition support services. For more information about the **Minnesota Workforce Centers**, see page 22.

AMERICAN INDIAN OIC

1845 E. Franklin Ave.
Minneapolis, MN 55404
(612) 341-3358

1915 Chicago Ave. So.
Minneapolis, MN 55404
(612) 879-8113

Targeted to Native Americans. Job-search coaching, vocational assessment, job bank, GED/basic skills preparation, daycare, training.

CAREER OPPORTUNITIES PREPARATION FOR EMPLOYMENT

Program of Family Service, Inc.

166 E. Fourth St., Suite 200, St. Paul, MN 55101
(612) 222-0311   Fax—(612) 222-8920

Open to the public. Career assessment, testing, job-search coaching, personalized counseling. Call for appointment. Adjusted fee scale.

▲ CARVER COUNTY EMPLOYMENT AND TRAINING CENTER

600 E. Fourth Street, Chaska, MN 55318
(612) 361-1600   Fax—(612) 361-1660

Open to the public but eligibility is based on residency, work location or income. Job-search coaching, testing, assessment, training, job leads. Free.

CENTER FOR ASIANS AND PACIFIC ISLANDERS

3702 E. Lake Street, Suite 101, Minneapolis, MN 55406
(612) 721-0122   Fax—(612) 721-7054

Serves refugees, economically disadvantaged youth and welfare recipients. Vocational assessment, job-search coaching, job club. Free.

▲ CENTER FOR EMPLOYMENT AND TRAINING

Program of St. Paul Public Schools

215 E. 9th Street, St. Paul, MN 55101
(612) 228-3284   Fax—(612) 292-7981

Open to youth and adults. Eligibility based on residency, work location or income. Job-search coaching, testing, assessment, training, job leads. Free.

▲ CENTER FOR CAREER CHANGE
Division of Metropolitan Senior Federation
1885 University Avenue
St. Paul, MN 55104
(612) 645-0261   Fax—(612) 641-8969

Open to individuals experiencing age discrimination in job search. Provides job-search counseling, job leads, pension information and retirement counseling. Call for an appointment. Sliding fee.

CLUES
Chicanos Latinos Unidos En Servicios
2110 Nicollet Ave. So.   220 So. Robert St., Suite 103
Minneapolis, MN 55404   St. Paul, MN 55107
(612) 871-0200   (612) 292-0117
Fax—(612) 871-1058   Fax—(612) 292-0347

Employment assistance targeted to Hispanics. Services include career assessment, testing, job-search coaching, job bank, workshops. Free.

▲ DAKOTA COUNTY EMPLOYMENT AND TRAINING CENTER
1300 145th St. East
Rosemount, MN 55068
(612) 423-6363   Fax—(612) 423-9706

Job-search coaching, assessment, testing, tuition for retraining, job leads, referrals to off-site employment programs. Eligibility for services based on residency, income or other criteria determined by program. Free.

▲ EAST SIDE NEIGHBORHOOD SERVICE, INC.
1929 Second St. N.E.
Minneapolis, MN 55418
(612) 781-6011   Fax—(612) 781-9257

Open to the public. Career counseling, job-seeking skills training, job leads. Job placement for low-income Hennepin County residents, age 55 and older. Call for appointment. Free to eligible participants.

EDUCATIONAL OPPORTUNITY CENTER
Program of U.S. Department of Education / TRIO Programs
1501 Hennepin Avenue
Minneapolis, MN 55403
(612) 349-2524   Fax—(612) 341-7075

Open to adults with less than a four-year college degree. Offers career planning, financial aid counseling. Helps research post-secondary schools. Fourteen metro-wide locations. Call for appointment. Free.

▲ EMPLOYMENT ACTION CENTER
Lenox Community Center, 6715 Minnetonka Blvd.
St. Louis Park, MN 55426
(612) 925-9195   Fax—(612) 924-1295

Open to the public. Assists unemployed, underemployed individuals in career transition. Employment and personal counseling, job-seeking skills, job placement. Call for program information. Free or low cost.

ETHIOPIANS IN MINNESOTA, INC.
1821 University Ave. W., Suite 321
St. Paul, MN 55104
(612) 645-4633   Fax—(612) 645-1073

Serves Ethiopian and other refugees receiving public assistance. Vocational assessment, testing, job bank, job-search coaching, mentorship program, job placement, training. Call for appointment. Free.

EXPANDED HORIZONS
Carver-Scott Educational Cooperative
401 E. Fourth Street
Chaska, MN 55318
(612) 448-1885   Fax—(612) 368-8858

Targeted to women on AFDC and others interested in training and employment. Career testing and exploration, assertiveness and self-esteem training, parenting skills. Free to eligible participants.

FAMILIES WORKING TOGETHER
Episcopal Community Services Inc.

1010 University Avenue
St. Paul, MN 55104
(612) 290-4760
Fax—(612) 290-4761

123 No. Third St., Suite 702
Minneapolis, MN 55401
(612) 341-2680
Fax—(612) 341-2760

215 North 4th Street
Stillwater, MN 55802
(612) 439-2641

Open to low income parents. Offers career planning, job-search counseling, workshops, on-site childcare, job leads, transportation assistance, interview clothing. Call for appointment. Free.

▲ GREATER MINNEAPOLIS CHAMBER OF COMMERCE

81 So. 9th St., Suite 200
Minneapolis, MN 55402
(612) 370-9160   Fax—(612) 370-9195

Targeted to low-income adults and youth. Adult program offers career and job-search counseling, educational counseling, job leads, financial assistance for daycare and transportation. Free.

▲ HENNEPIN COUNTY DEPARTMENT OF TRAINING AND EMPLOYMENT ASSISTANCE

Hennepin County Government Center First Level So.
300 So. Sixth St.
Minneapolis, MN 55487
(612) 348-7003—General information
(612) 348-9023—Dislocated Worker Program Info Hotline

Government supervisory agency. Administers funding for employment programs for residents of suburban Hennepin County (dislocated workers, people of low income and families on public assistance).

▲ HIRED

1200 Plymouth Ave. No.
Minneapolis, MN 55411
(612) 529-3342
Fax—(612) 529-7131

Sabathani Center
310 E. 38th Street
Minneapolis, MN 55409
(612) 822-9071

Griggs Midway Bldg., Ste. N170
1821 W. University Ave.
St. Paul, MN 55104
(612) 647-5620

Robbinsdale Center
4139 Regent Ave. No.
Robbinsdale, MN 55422
(612) 536-0777

Open to the public. Career and job-search counseling, resume development, coaching for networking and interviewing. Provides resource library, training opportunities, job leads and HIRED's Job Link, an electronic database of job listings. Eligibility varies. Call for appointment. Free.

▲ HTC EMPLOYMENT AND TRAINING PROGRAMS

7145 Harriet Ave. So.
Richfield, MN 55423
(612) 861-7481   Fax—(612) 866-2304

Employment services for residents of suburban Hennepin County. Career testing, assessment, job-seeking skills, job leads, retraining, resource library, workshops. Eligibility based on residency and income. Free or low cost.

JEWISH FAMILY SERVICE

790 So. Cleveland Ave., Suite 227
St. Paul, MN 55116
(612) 698-0767   Fax—(612) 698-0162
E-mail: gseaks@winternet.com

Open to the public. Offers career assessment, workshops, resume preparation, job bank, job club, job placement, job leads and job-search coaching including videotaped interviewing, job support group, computer and internet access. Call for appointment. Sliding fee.

JEWISH VOCATIONAL SERVICE

1500 So. Highway 100, Suite 311
Minneapolis, MN 55416
(612) 591-0300   Fax—(612) 591-0227

Open to the public. Job-finding strategies, career and educational counseling, assistance expanding networks, resource library, workshops. Also offers job skills training, assessment and job placement to people facing barriers to employment. Flexible rates.

LA OPORTUNIDAD

1821 University Ave. W., Suite 5157
St. Paul, MN 55104
(612) 646-6115   Fax—(612) 646-7564

Serves Hispanic offenders and ex-offenders. Vocational assessment, testing, job-search coaching, interviewing help, job leads, workshops, support groups. Call for appointment. Free.

LAO FAMILY COMMUNITY OF MINNESOTA

320 W. University Ave.
St. Paul, MN 55103
(612) 221-0069   Fax—(612) 221-0276

Targeted to members of Hmong community. Career assessment, job-search coaching, resume assistance, job bank, workshops. Literacy and youth employment programs. Call for appointment. Some services have eligibility requirements. Free.

LIFEWORKS MOBILE JOB BANK

8900 Portland Avenue So.
Bloomington, MN 55420
(612) 885-8525   Fax—(612) 885-8437

Open to the public. Provides job placement, retraining, job leads, referrals to other programs and job-search coaching including interviewing skills. Call for appointment. Free.

▲ LORING NICOLLET-BETHLEHEM COMMUNITY CENTER, INC.

1925 Nicollet Ave. So.
Minneapolis, MN 55403
(612) 871-2031   Fax—(612) 871-8121

Serves adults and youth. Focuses on education and employment. Career assessment, job-search counseling, resume assistance, job leads. Call for an appointment. Free to eligible participants.

▲ MINNEAPOLIS EMPLOYMENT AND TRAINING PROGRAM

350 So. Fifth St., Room 310-1/2 City Hall
Minneapolis, MN 55415
(612) 673-5700   Fax—(612) 673-2108

Government supervisory agency. Provides government funding and referrals to employment programs offered at Minneapolis neighborhood centers. Free to eligible participants. Call for information and referrals.

▲ MINNEAPOLIS URBAN LEAGUE EMPLOYMENT & TRAINING

2000 Plymouth Ave. No.
Minneapolis, MN 55411
(612) 521-0342   Fax—(612) 521-8513

Open to the public but primarily serves Minneapolis residents. Assists with job-seeking/keeping skills, transportation allowance, referrals for training, job leads. Free to eligible participants.

▲ MINNESOTA MAINSTREAM

Division of RISE, Inc.

8406 Sunset Road N.E.
Spring Lake Park, MN 55432
(612) 786-8334   Fax—(612) 786-0008

Open to unemployed with bachelor's degree recovering from mental illness. Must be referred by Minnesota Div. of Rehab Services. Career and job-search coaching, mentorship program. Free to eligible participants.

NORTH CENTRAL CAREER DEVELOPMENT CENTER

516 Mission House Lane
New Brighton, MN 55112
(612) 636-5120   Fax—(612) 636-5124

Open to the public but targeted to church professionals. Provides career assessment, testing, workshops, resource library and job-search coaching including interviewing skills. Call for appointment. $400/basic package.

▲ PHILLIPS COMMUNITY DEVELOPMENT CORP.

1014 E. Franklin Avenue
Minneapolis, MN 55404
(612) 871-2122—Job Bank
(612) 871-2435—Economic Development
Fax—(612) 871-8131

Primarily serves Phillips community. Career testing, assessment, job-search assistance, vocational training, job leads. Program for entrepreneurs with grants and loans available. Free.

▲ PILLSBURY NEIGHBORHOOD SERVICES, INC.

UNITY CENTER
2507 Fremont Ave. No.
Minneapolis, MN 55411
(612) 529-9267
Fax—(612) 529-4743

COYLE CENTER
420 15th Avenue So.
Minneapolis, MN 55454
(612) 338-5282

Serves Minneapolis adults and youth. Assistance with job-readiness skills, job leads, interest and aptitude testing. Training assistance may be available. Call for appointment. Free to eligible participants.

For an explanation of this symbol ▲ see page 29.

▲ PROJECT SELF-SUFFICIENCY
Minneapolis Public Housing Authority

600 18th Ave. No.
Minneapolis, MN 55411
(612) 342-1360   Fax—(612) 342-1367

Employment and training assistance, counseling, advocacy and job link
service for matching people to jobs. Free to eligible participants.

▲ PROJECT TURNAROUND
Loring Nicollet Bethlehem Community Centers Inc.

1925 Nicollet Avenue So.
Minneapolis, MN 55403
(612) 871-2031   Fax—(612) 871-8121

Open only to ex-offenders/felons. Helps find transitional employment
soon after release. Career assessment, testing, job bank, resource library,
job leads and coaching. Referrals to community resources. Free.

▲ RAMSEY COUNTY OIC
Opportunities Industrialization Center, Inc.

800 East Minnehaha Ave.
St. Paul, MN 55106
(612) 771-3008   Fax—(612) 771-1413

Targeted to unemployed/underemployed who meet poverty guidelines.
Testing, job-search coaching, job placement, vocational training,
GED/basic skills. Lending library of interview clothing. Sliding fee scale.

▲ RISE, INC.

8406 Sunset Road N.E.
Spring Lake Park, MN 55432
(612) 786-8334   Fax—(612) 786-0008

Targeted to individuals with disabilities. Job-search coaching, training,
placement, follow-up, support services. Free to eligible participants.

▲ ST. PAUL LABOR STUDIES

Workforce Development Center, 215 East 9th Street
St. Paul, MN 55101
(612) 228-3283   Fax—(612) 228-3299

Serves east metro residents who have lost jobs due to layoffs and plant closings. Career planning, full-service job-search counseling. Job leads, crisis assistance. Free to eligible participants.

▲ ST. PAUL URBAN LEAGUE

401 Selby Avenue
St. Paul, MN 55102
(612) 224-5771   Fax—(612) 224-8009

Targeted to minorities and disadvantaged individuals. Provides career planning, job-search counseling, resource library, interest/career testing, job leads. Eligibility varies by program. Free.

▲ SCOTT COUNTY HUMAN SERVICES

Court House 300, 428 So. Holmes Street
Shakopee, MN 55370
(612) 445-7751   Fax—(612) 496-8430

Eligibility based on residency, work location or income. Career planning, job-search coaching, testing, training, job leads, placement, educational counseling. Referrals to off-site programs. Call for appointment. Free.

▲ SUBURBAN PATHWAYS

Program of Employment Action Center

6715 Minnetonka Blvd., Suite 205
St. Louis Park, MN 55426
(612) 924-1273   Fax—(612) 924-1295

Open to recipients of AFDC in Hennepin County. Job-search assistance, job placement, internships, training. Self-esteem workshops, childcare, transportation assistance. Free.

TAPS
Training Applicants for Placement Success

777 Raymond Avenue
St. Paul, MN 55114
(612) 646-8675   (800) 779-0777   Fax—(612) 646-1887

For individuals with epilepsy, age 16 and up. Job-search coaching, resume help, job club, job leads, epilepsy education. Call for appointment. Free.

THE CITY, INC.

1545 E. Lake Street
Minneapolis, MN 55407
(612) 724-3689
Fax—(612) 724-0692

1315 12th Ave. No.
Minneapolis, MN 55411
(612) 377-7559

Employment programs targeted to youth, adults, African-Americans and Native Americans. Vocational assessment, testing, job-search skills, resource library, job bank, job support group. Call for appointment. Free.

UNITED CAMBODIAN ASSOCIATION OF MINNESOTA

529 Jackson St., Room 221
St. Paul, MN 55101
(612) 222-3299   Fax—(612) 222-3599

Targeted to Cambodian community. Vocational assessment, job-search coaching, job placement, workshops, job club. Call for appointment. Free.

VET CENTER

2480 University Avenue
St. Paul, MN 55114
(612) 644-4022   Fax—(612) 725-2234

Individual and group re-adjustment counseling to Vietnam-era and post-combat veterans since the Vietnam War. Job-search assistance, job leads, support groups open to all veterans. Call for appointment or drop in. Free.

▲ WINGS
Program of Employment Action Center

3200 Penn Avenue No.
Minneapolis, MN 55412
(612) 521-8750
Fax—(612) 521-3818

1527 E. Lake St., 2nd Floor
Minneapolis, MN 55407
(612) 721-2714
Fax—(612) 721-4347

Open to recipients of AFDC who meet residency requirements. Job-search assistance, job placement, internships, training, workshops. Childcare and transportation assistance. Call for appointment. Free.

▲ WOMEN ACHIEVING NEW DIRECTIONS
Program of Employment Action Center

3200 Penn Avenue No.
Minneapolis, MN 55412
(612) 521-1232—Minneapolis residents
(612) 225-0888—St. Paul residents
Fax—(612) 521-3818

Open to low- or single-income working mothers. Job-search and job-promotion counseling, interest and aptitude testing, resource library, workshops and job leads. Call for information or to schedule an appointment. Free or low cost.

▲ WOMEN IN TRANSITION
Program of Employment Action Center

6715 Minnetonka Blvd.
St. Louis Park, MN 55426
(612) 924-1266
Fax—(612) 924-1295

Targeted to women. Services include career planning, full-service job-search counseling, resource library, interest and career testing, job placement and self-esteem workshops. Call for information or appointment. Sliding fee.

For an explanation of this symbol ▲ *see page 29.*

TWIN CITIES

▲ WOMEN'S EMPLOYMENT RESOURCE CENTER
Program of Catholic Charities

2104 Stevens Ave. So.	1276 University Avenue
Minneapolis, MN 55404	St. Paul, MN 55104
(612) 872-8777	(612) 641-1180
Fax—(612) 872-9696	Fax—(612) 641-1005

Open to low-income women. Seven-week job-search preparation assistance. Career assessment, resume preparation, job application tips, interview training, mentoring opportunities, job placement. Free.

WOMENVENTURE

2324 University Ave. W., Suite 200
St. Paul, MN 55114
(612) 646-3808   Fax—(612) 641-7223

Services for women and men of all ages. Career assessment/planning, individual career consulting, workshops, support group and resource library. Help with business start-up or growth. Free or sliding fee.

WORKING OPPORTUNITIES FOR WOMEN

2700 University W., Suite 12
St. Paul, MN 55114
(612) 647-9961   Fax—(612) 647-1424

Assistance with employment goal setting, individualized career and job-search coaching, resource library, workshops. Also provides convenient telephone counseling option. Call for appointment. Free or low cost.

YOUTH EXPRESS

1429 Marshall Avenue
St. Paul, MN 55104
(612) 659-0613   Fax—(612) 659-0613

Targeted to St. Paul youth, age 12-17. Job referral service. Provides job leads, resume help and job coaching. Call for appointment. Participant must perform community service projects. Free.

▲ ARROWHEAD ECONOMIC OPPORTUNITY AGENCY

Open to residents of Aitkin, Carlton, Cook, Itasca, Koochiching, Lake, St. Louis Counties. Services include career assessment, testing, job-search coaching, resume and interview preparation, resource library. Job leads, retraining. Call for appointment. Fees vary.

MAIN OFFICE
702 Third Ave. So.
Virginia, MN 55792
(218) 749-2912
(800) 662-5711

AITKIN
210 Second St. N.W.
Aitkin, MN 56431
(218) 927-7046

CLOQUET
30 No. 10th Street
Cloquet, MN 55720
(218) 879-5201

DULUTH
5702 Miller Trunk Highway
Duluth, MN 55811
(218) 729-5509

ELY COMMUNITY CENTER
30 So. First Ave. East
Ely, MN 55731
(218) 365-3359

GRAND MARAIS
P.O. Box 331
Grand Marais, MN 55604
(218) 387-1134

GRAND RAPIDS
421 S.E. 13th Street
Grand Rapids, MN 55744
(218) 327-1138

HIBBING
c/o Stuntz Garage
1100 E. 25th Street
Hibbing, MN 55746
(218) 263-5513

INTERNATIONAL FALLS
Forestland Annex, Lower Level
1000 5th Street
International Falls, MN 56649
(218) 283-3478

TWO HARBORS
c/o The Depot
520 South Avenue
Two Harbors, MN 55616
(218) 834-2280
(800) 223-1850

For an explanation of this symbol ▲ see page 29.

▲ EMPLOYMENT AND TRAINING CENTER

Pine Technical College, 1100 Fourth Street
Pine City, MN 55063
(320) 629-6741   (800) 633-7284   Fax—(320) 629-7603

Open and free to participants of specific government funded programs.
Career assessment, testing, job-search coaching, workshops, job leads.

▲ FLEXWORK

Program of RESOURCE, Inc.

Midtown Square
3333 W. Division St.
St. Cloud, MN 56301
(320) 259-5717
Fax—(320) 259-7066

205 W. Second St., Suite 444
Duluth, MN 55802
(218) 722-9700
Fax—(218) 722-9724

Job placement for disabled and minorities. Job-search coaching, skills
training. Must be referred by the Division of Rehabilitation Services, State
Services for the Blind or other third party. Free to eligible individuals.

FUNCTIONAL INDUSTRIES, INC.

Sher-Wright Employment Program

1801 Highway 25
Buffalo, MN 55313
(612) 682-4336   Fax—(612) 682-4336

Open only to residents of Sherburne/Wright Counties with serious and
persistent mental illness. Job placement, resume help, job leads. Free.

GREEN THUMB, INC.

P.O. Box 310, Wadena, MN 56482
(218) 631-3483   (800) 450-5627   Fax—(218) 631-3077

Open to individuals, age 55 and older, with limited incomes. On-site job
training and placement in community and private sector settings. Call for
locations in 62 rural Minnesota counties. Free.

LIFE-WORK PLANNING CENTER
Nichols Center, 410 Jackson
Mankato, MN 56001
(507) 345-1577   Fax—(507) 234-1469

For women in transition. Career assessment, testing, workshops, job-search coaching, resource library, job leads. Computer access, support groups, entrepreneur groups. Bilingual (Spanish-English). Free to eligible participants.

LUTHERAN SOCIAL SERVICES
Counseling Center

600 Ordean Building, 424 W. Superior Street
Duluth, MN 55802
(218) 726-4769   Fax—(218) 726-1251

Open to the public. Services include career assessment, testing, individual counseling. Call for information and fees.

MAINSTAY, INC.
308 No. Third Street
Marshall, MN 56258
(507) 537-1546   (800) 554-2481   Fax—(507) 537-4550

Targeted to individuals in southwestern Minnesota. Resume development, interviewing skills, vocational assessment, job-search coaching, workshops, placement, small business counseling, resource library. First appointment free.

▲ NON-TRADITIONAL EMPLOYMENT FOR WOMEN
Northwest Private Industry Council

721 So. Minnesota Street
Crookston, MN 56716
(218) 281-5180   Fax—(218) 281-5185

Targeted to women in, or seeking employment in, non-traditional fields. Offers career assessment, classroom and work training. Assistance with daycare and transportation. Free to eligible participants.

For an explanation of this symbol ▲ see page 29.   **45**

▲ NORTHEAST MINNESOTA OFFICE OF JOB TRAINING

Call for locations in Cloquet, Duluth, Grand Rapids, Hibbing, International Falls and Virginia.

820 No. 9th Street, Suite 240
P.O. Box 1028
Virginia, MN 55792
(218) 749-1274   (800) 325-5332   Fax—(218) 749-1673

Open only to eligible participants. Services include career assessment and testing, workshops, job bank, assistance with resumes and interviewing, resource library, job coaching. Free.

NORTHWEST INDIAN OIC

1819 Bemidji Avenue No.
Bemidji, MN 56601
(218) 759-2022

Targeted to Native Americans. Services include vocational assessment, testing, job-search coaching, help with resumes and interviewing, skills enhancement (GED), job placement. Also offers Walks Tall program, a pre- and post-release service for American Indian offenders in the State Department of Corrections. Drop in. Free.

OJIBWA EMPLOYMENT & TRAINING CENTER
White Earth Reservation Tribal Council

Box 37, Waubun, MN 56589
(218) 473-2141   (800) 726-8951
Fax—(218) 473-2186
E-mail: Ojibwa@White.Earth.CFA.org

Open to Native Americans who are economically disadvantaged or AFDC recipients. Provides vocational assessment, testing, resume assistance, job leads, retraining. Classroom and on-the-job training, childcare assistance. Call for appointment. Free.

OLMSTED COMMUNITY ACTION PROGRAM

1421 Third Ave. S.E.
Rochester, MN 55904
(507) 285-8785
Fax—(507) 285-8401

Employment assistance, free to eligible participants. Services include career assessment, testing and job-search coaching. Call for information about eligibility requirements.

OPPORTUNITY TRAINING CENTER, INC.

318 14th Ave. No.
St. Cloud, MN 56302
(320) 252-2651

614 West Central Street
Detroit Lakes, MN 56501
(218) 847-3080

1119 Madison Street
Brainerd, MN 56401
(218) 828-4321

518 Lincoln Road, Box 201
Sauk Centre, MN 56378
(320) 352-3604

706 Ash Avenue N.W.
Wadena, MN 56482
(218) 631-4933

For individuals with barriers to employment. Third party referral required. Offers vocational evaluation, training, and job placement assistance. Call for information, eligibility and fees.

▲ PRIVATE INDUSTRY COUNCIL 5

500 Elm St. East
P.O. Box 579
Annandale, MN 55302
(320) 274-2650   (800) 284-7425   Fax—(320) 274-3516

Employment assistance, free to eligible participants of government funded programs. Provides career assessment, testing, resume preparation, job leads, job bank, workshops. Call for appointment.

PROJECT SOAR

205 W. Second Street
Duluth, MN 55812
(218) 722-3126   Fax—(218) 722-4617

Helps women at all economic levels to achieve personal strength and financial self-sufficiency. Employment and education counseling, testing, assessment, advocacy and resume development. Call for appointment.

▲ RURAL MINNESOTA CEP, INC.

Open to the public but certain programs have eligibility requirements. Employment planning, job-search workshops, funding for post-secondary education, on-the-job training, work programs. Free to eligible participants.

ADMINISTRATIVE OFFICE

803 Roosevelt Avenue
Detroit Lakes, MN 56502
(218) 847-9205   (800) 492-4804

BEMIDJI

1008 Washington Ave. So.
P.O. Box 1690
Bemidji, MN 56619
(218) 751-8012   (800) 569-4196

BRAINERD

1919 So. 6th St., P.O. Box 528
Brainerd, MN 56401
(218) 828-6186   (800) 664-3595

DETROIT LAKES

801 Roosevelt Avenue
Detroit Lakes, MN 56502
(218) 847-2101
(800) 492-4810

MOORHEAD

Family Service Center
715 No. 11th St., Suite 302
Moorhead, MN 56560
(218) 233-1541

STAPLES

616 North 4th Street
Staples, MN 56479
(218) 894-3771

FERGUS FALLS

118 So. Mill St., Suite 302
Fergus Falls, MN 56537
(218) 736-6963
(800) 710-6923

LITTLE FALLS

109 6th Street N.E.
Little Falls, MN 56345
(320) 632-2356

▲ S.E. MINNESOTA PRIVATE INDUSTRY COUNCIL, INC.

300 11th Ave. N.W., Suite 110
Rochester, MN 55901
(507) 281-1193
(800) 543-5627
Fax—(507) 252-2470

Targeted to dislocated and low-income individuals. Career assessment, testing, job-search coaching, job leads. Computer and life skills training, welding and machining classes. Math and English updating. Drop in. Free.

▲ S.W. MINNESOTA PRIVATE INDUSTRY COUNCIL

Call for locations in Worthington and Montevideo.
1424 E. College Dr., Suite 100
Marshall, MN 56258
(507) 532-4411   (800) 422-0687
Fax—(507) 532-4703

Employment assistance, free to eligible participants of government funded programs. Career assessment, job-search coaching, job leads. On-the-job and classroom training. Relocation, daycare and transportation assistance. Call for appointment.

▲ STEARNS-BENTON EMPLOYMENT & TRAINING COUNCIL

3333 W. Division
P.O. Box 615
St. Cloud, MN 56302
(320) 656-3990
Fax—(320) 202-2100

Open to the public but eligibility requirements vary by program. Services include career assessment and testing, workshops, job club, resource library, job-search coaching, resume and interview preparation and customized skill training. Call for appointment or drop in. Free to those who meet eligibility requirements.

STEPPING STONES

Heartland Community Action

Willmar Family Learning Center
1108 Hwy. 71 North
Willmar, MN 56201
(320) 235-0850 or (320) 235-6661
Fax—(320) 235-7703

Targeted to divorced or separated individuals who have lost their means
of support. Services include career assessment, testing, resume
preparation, job-search coaching, resource library. Call for appointment.
Sliding fee. Free to low-income individuals.

WINGS

700 W. Germain Street
St. Cloud, MN 56301
(320) 251-1612

Open to women who have lost their means of support. Services provided
through 12-week workshops. Weekly training in self-confidence, esteem
building, interviewing skills, resume development. Call for appointment.
Free to eligible participants.

CAREER COACHING

SERVICES

PRIVATE SECTOR

In this section you'll find career experts from the private sector who specialize in serving managers, professionals, executives and other individuals in job transition or mid-life career change.

◆ For some folks, private sector resources make good sense. Although often, but not always, more expensive than non profits, the business-like environment and selection of services may be appealing.

◆ Several firms offer amenities like office space, secretarial services, access to computers and the Internet and fully-stocked resource centers. But these extras do not come cheap. Some services charge $3,000 or more for a full-service job coaching package. On the other hand, smaller firms or individual career professionals may offer group services, or charge by the hour or project, at a much less expensive rate.

◆ The consideration of fees is especially important in this section where costs can add up. Before you make any financial commitments, research the company thoroughly. Ask for references and credentials.

◆ Watch out for pricey one-size-fits-all packages that require advance payment. If you really only want some quick tips to re-charge your search or feedback on your resume, a full battery of career tests or other extras may be overkill for your needs and budget.

GUIDELINES FOR SELECTING A CAREER COUNSELOR

Prepared by the National Career Development Association

◆ Ask the counselor for a detailed explanation of services—career counseling, testing, employment search strategy planning and resume writing—he or she provides. Make sure you understand the service, your degree of involvement and financial commitment.

◆ Select a counselor who is professionally trained and will let you choose the services you desire. Make certain you can terminate the services at any time, paying only for services rendered.

◆ Be skeptical of services that make promises of more money, better jobs, resumes that get speedier results or an immediate solution to career problems. Professional codes of ethics by such organizations as the **National Career Development Association, American Counseling Association** and **American Psychological Association**, advise against grandiose guarantees and promises, exorbitant fees and breaches of confidentiality, among other things.

◆ Ask for a detailed explanation of services offered, your financial and time commitments and a copy of the ethical guidelines used by the career counselor you're considering. For a free copy of **"Code of Ethics and Standards of Practice"** published by the American Counseling Association, call (800) 347-6647.

Please note: There are many experienced career professionals in this community but, at the present time in Minnesota, there is no competency-based system for licensing career counselors. That means that anyone can enter into the business of "career consulting" without first having met any minimum level of education or training. For that reason, it's wise to be a careful and intelligent consumer.

ADVICE...

7964 Brooklyn Blvd., Suite 112
Brooklyn Park, MN 55445
(612) 560-2223   Fax—(612) 560-2214

Provides career assessment, testing, workshops, resume preparation and job-search coaching including interviewing skills. Call for appointment and fees.

ALL-PROFESSIONAL CAREER MANAGEMENT

1550 E. 79th St., Suite 680
Bloomington, MN 55425
(612) 854-7705   Fax—(612) 854-9521

Services include career planning, testing, individualized and group counseling. Emphasis on interview preparation. Provides resource library, support groups. Call for appointment. Fees vary by project.

ALLEN AND ASSOCIATES

6600 France Avenue So.
Edina, MN 55435
(612) 925-9646   (800) 562-7925   Fax—(612) 925-9662

Offers job-search coaching, career assessment, resume preparation, marketing letters and database of employers. Also provides mailing and answering services, office space, resource library and reference checking. Call for appointment and fees.

ASSOCIATED CAREER SERVICES, INC.

3585 Lexington Avenue No., Suite 205
Arden Hills, MN 55126
(612) 787-0501   Fax—(612) 787-0807

Services include career planning, assessment and resume development. Also provides resource library and computerized career exploration. Fees are hourly or based on services required. Call for appointment.

BARBARA PARKS AND ASSOCIATES

4134 Park Ave.
Minneapolis, MN 55407
(612) 822-0288

Offers career assessment, testing, workshops, resource library, resume preparation and job-search coaching including interviewing/salary negotiation skills. Also provides career and lifework consulting. Call for appointment and fees. Free initial consultation.

BETTER LIFE CHOICES

12450 Wayzata Blvd., Suite 224
Minnetonka, MN 55305
(612) 649-4837

Career services include coaching in job-search and interviewing skills. Assists with approaches to tap the hidden job market. Also offers workshops. Call for appointment. Sliding fee scale.

BILEK CONSULTING

4640 W. 77th St., Suite 310
Edina, MN 55435
(612) 832-0557   Fax—(612) 835-4372

Coaching in strategic market positioning and job-search skills. Also offers outplacement services, workshops, career assessment, testing, international employment services and resource library. Call for information.

CAREER MANAGEMENT SERVICES

333 Washington Ave. No., Suite 300
Minneapolis, MN 55401
(612) 373-7013   Fax—(612) 349-2760

Targeted to the legal profession. Provides career assessment and testing, job-search coaching including interviewing and salary negotiation skills, resume preparation, resource library. Call for information and appointment. Sliding fee.

CENTER FOR COUNSELING AND STRESS MANAGEMENT

1204 Harmon Place
Minneapolis, MN 55403
(612) 333-1766   Fax—(612) 333-1784

Career development assistance by licensed psychologist. Services include testing, assessment, assistance with career decision-making and job-search strategies. Call for appointment. Sliding fee scale.

COLLEEN CONVEY AND ASSOCIATES

2636 Lyndale Ave. So., Suite 212
Minneapolis, MN 55408
(612) 870-4911

Offers career assessment, testing, workshops, job-search coaching including interviewing/salary negotiation skills, resume coaching. Call for appointment. $75 for 90-minute session.

CRAIG GROUP INTERNATIONAL

Highway 169 and Anderson Lakes Parkway
Eden Prairie, MN 55344-3910
Phone/Fax—(612) 944-1759

Specializes in assisting with career change including identifying transferrable skills. Offers individual/group career consulting, resume broadcast letters/cover letters, assistance with goal-setting and job-search strategy. Also provides help in utilizing the hidden job market and videotaped interview coaching. Call for appointment and fees.

C R CONSULTING, INC.

151 Silver Lake Road
New Brighton, MN 55112
(612) 633-6727   Fax—(612) 631-2116

Provides career assessment, testing, resume preparation and job-search coaching including interviewing skills. Specializes in serving those with non-traditional lifestyles. Call for appointment. $30-65/hour.

DREAMGROWERS

900 W. 128th Street, Suite 208
Burnsville, MN 55337
(612) 894-2915   Fax—(612) 894-7119

Provides evaluation of individual skills, exploration of alternative work options. Assists with targeting objectives, development of individual job-search plan, resumes, briefs and portfolios. Free initial consultation.

DRI CONSULTING

7715 Stonewood Court
Edina, MN 55439
(612) 941-9656   Fax—(612) 941-2693
Internet address: http://www.dric.com
E-mail: dric@dric.com

Organizational and career psychologists/consultants provide career testing, marketing and job-search support to individuals and organizations. Free initial consultation.

JOB FIT ENTERPRISES

6279 Bury Drive
Eden Prairie, MN 55345
(612) 949-8638   Fax—(612) 949-2715

Career planning service helps clients evaluate personal qualities to explore careers with a high job-fit potential. Free initial consultation.

KURENITZ & ASSOCIATES

5851 Duluth Street, Suite 115
Golden Valley, MN 55422
(612) 513-5941   Fax—(612) 513-5937

Assists in career/life planning and provides job transition services such as goal-setting, interview assistance, resume construction, job-search strategies. Fees are hourly or on a project basis. Free initial consultation.

LIFE DIMENSIONS, INC.

3060 Magnolia No.
Minneapolis, MN 55441-2858
(612) 559-1177   Fax—(612) 559-2160

Provides strategies for work transitions and job search. Facilitates career/life management groups for career focusing and goal setting. Special services include relocation support through the National Network of Career and Life Management Consultants. Call for appointment and fees.

LOFTUS BROWN-WESCOTT, INC.

Kickernick Bldg., Suite 790
430 First Ave. No.
Minneapolis, MN 55401
(612) 341-1024   Fax—(612) 338-5436

Assistance with employment goal-setting and strategies, industry and job research. Call for appointment. Fees vary by services required.

MARKET SHARE INC.

155 Fifth Ave. So., Suite 350
Minneapolis, MN 55401
(612) 375-9277   Fax—(612) 334-5727

Manager-level coaching in career assessment, marketing strategies, employer research, entrepreneurial planning. Also provides resource library. Office space available. Call for appointment and fees.

PATHFINDER PERSONNEL SERVICES, INC.

708 No. First St., Suite 244
Minneapolis, MN 55401
Phone/Fax—(612) 333-5944

Provides a variety of assessment tests and guided exploration of job opportunities and employment alternatives. Assistance and training with resume/letter-writing, interviewing, telephone contact skills, networking and job leads. Call for appointment. Hourly fees and package programs.

PATRICIA SCOTT AND ASSOCIATES

4628 Zenith Ave. So.
Minneapolis, MN 55410
(612) 925-1866

Offers career assessment, testing, resume preparation and job-search coaching. Also provides workshops, resource library and networking groups. Call for appointment and fees.

PDI / MEREDITH / LINCOLNSHIRE INTERNATIONAL

7760 France Ave. So., Suite 750
Minneapolis, MN 55435
(612) 921-0400   Fax—(612) 921-1633

Assistance with goal-setting and strategizing, personal marketing, resume development. Also provides office space, secretarial services, resource library, Internet access, support groups, job leads. Call for appointment and fees.

PROTOTYPE CAREER SERVICES

626 Armstrong Ave.
St. Paul, MN 55102
(612) 224-2856   (800) 368-3197   Fax—(612) 224-5526

Targeted to workers who have lost their jobs due to layoffs. One-to-one consulting, resume assistance, videotaped interview coaching, employer and career research. Also offers job-search workshops, evening/weekend appointments. Hourly fees. Two Twin Cities locations.

PSYCHOLOGICAL AND CAREER CONSULTANTS

3232 Buchanan Street N.E.
Minneapolis, MN 55418
(612) 789-9596   Fax—(612) 789-4979

Services include career assessment, testing, resume preparation, job-search coaching and assistance with interviewing and salary negotiation skills. Also offers job leads and workshops. Call for appointment and fees.

RESOURCE PUBLISHING GROUP INC.

P.O. Box 573
Hopkins, MN 55343
(612) 545-5980   (800) 555-9058   Fax—(612) 545-9241
Minnesota Career Store: http://www.careerstore.com
E-Mail: RPG@primenet.com

Publisher of unique resources and tools for Minnesotans and others in career and workplace transition including: *Minnesota Job Seeker's Sourcebook,* Twin Cities Job Seeker's Calendar, Job Search Resource Series and Quickstart Tool Kits. Also provides corporate outplacement services and workplace resources. Sponsor of the Minnesota Career Store, an online gateway to a sampler edition of the Job Seeker's Calendar, job tips, resources for job seekers and links to related Web sites. Call for information.

RICHARD E. ANDREA, Ph.D.
Licensed Psychologist / Nationally Certified Career Counselor

1399 Geneva Ave., Suite 201
Oakdale, MN 55128
(612) 738-6600
E-mail: randrea195@aol.com

Services include career counseling and testing, job-seeking skills training and personal counseling for job-related conflicts. Also provides career resource library with occupational and educational information. Call for information or appointment. Hourly or package fees.

SORENSEN & ASSOCIATES, INC.

5353 Wayzata Blvd., Suite 403
St. Louis Park, MN 55416
(612) 525-8161
Fax—(612) 544-7841

Broad range of career transition services including career assessment, assistance with goal setting and job-search marketing. Call for appointment. Fees are based on services required.

SQUARE ONE NATURAL GIFT TESTING CENTER

5620 Smetana Drive, Suite 120
Minneapolis, MN 55343
(612) 938-8367   Fax—(612) 938-4647

Career assessment, testing, in-depth aptitude assessment, workshops, resource library. Call for free consultation. $595/basic package.

STRATEGIES UNLIMITED

715 Florida Ave. So., Suite 406
Golden Valley, MN 55426
Phone/Fax—(612) 591-0936

Targeted to professionals and managers. Career assessment, testing, workshops, resume preparation, videotaped interviewing, job-search coaching including interviewing and salary negotiation skills. Also provides job leads and resource library. Call for appointment and fees.

TECHNICAL CAREER MANAGEMENT CONSULTANTS

1660 So. Highway 100, Suite 122
St. Louis Park, MN 55416
(612) 690-2755   Fax—(612) 699-6874 or (612) 591-1086
E-mail: dave@2000net.net

Targeted to professional and technical personnel. Provides career assessment, testing, resume preparation, assistance with interviewing and salary negotiations. Also offers job club, resource library and workshops. Call for appointment and fees.

THE ESQUIRE GROUP

430 First Ave. No., Suite 630
Minneapolis, MN 55401
(612) 340-9068   Fax—(612) 340-1218

Targeted to attorneys and professionals. Provides job-search and career advancement coaching, resume preparation, career assessment and testing, workshops. Call for appointment and fees.

VISIONARY GROWTH RESOURCES

16951 Island Avenue
Lakeville, MN 55044
(612) 898-1775   Fax—(612) 898-1776

Targeted to managerial, professional and recent college grads. Offers career assessment, testing, resume preparation, job-search coaching and network building skills. Also provides job leads and workshops. Call for appointment. Sliding fee.

WHITE PROFESSIONAL SERVICES INC.

(612) 754-5995

Offers career assessment/testing, workshops, resume preparation, job-search coaching, mass mailings and fax/printing/copying services. Also offers Internet access, resource library. Call for appointment. $60/hour.

WILLETTE WUNDERLIN LLC.

Parkdale One, 5401 Gamble Dr., Suite 250
Minneapolis, MN 55416
(612) 546-2285   Fax—(612) 546-1355

Provides vocational testing, job-search coaching and occupational stress management. Services provided by doctoral level licensed psychologists with management consulting and organizational development experience. Call for appointment and fees.

WORK/LIFE TRANSITIONS

620 Mendelssohn Ave. No., Suite 168
Golden Valley, MN 55427
(612) 544-4580   (800) 760-9997   Fax—(612) 544-4601
E-mail: WorkLifeT@aol.com

Services include assistance in career assessment, employment goal-setting and strategy, resume development, coaching to improve networking, interviewing and negotiation skills. Offers resource library, on-going support. Call for appointment. Free initial meeting. Hourly and package fees.

GREATER MINNESOTA

CAREER ADVANCEMENT SERVICES

620 Missabe Building
Duluth, MN 55802
(218) 722-0619

Services include resume preparation, job-search coaching and assistance with the development of business plans. Also provides job leads and access to career resource library. Referrals made to career assessment and testing services. Call for appointment and fees.

COMPLETE CAREER SERVICES

325 33rd Ave. No.
St. Cloud, MN 56303
(320) 255-0685
Fax—(320) 656-1564

1100 Hwy 210 W., Suite 2
Baxter, MN 56401
(218) 825-7008

Specializes in providing career services to the public and job placement services to injured workers. Services include career testing, assistance with resume-writing and job-search coaching. Call for appointment. Hourly fees start at $50.

DONOVAN & ASSOCIATES

Gary L. Donovan
1002 W. Fourth Street
Morris, MN 56267
(320) 589-4648 or (320) 589-6065

Nationally certified career counselor/licensed psychologist provides broad range of services including career assessment, testing and interpretation. Also offers job-search coaching and support, workshops and assistance with job placement. Call for appointment or information. Sliding fee scale.

GREATER MINNESOTA

LIFE DEVELOPMENT COUNSELING

CROSSROAD HOUSE
331 Dillon Ave.
Mankato, MN 56001
(507) 625-6862
Fax—(507) 389-4119

EDUCATION CENTER
151 Good Counsel Drive
Mankato, MN 56001
(507) 625-6862

Specializes in assisting with life and career planning. Services include career assessment and testing, job-search coaching and workshops. Call for information. Sliding fee.

ROCHESTER CAREER COUNSELING CENTER

Rochester, MN 55904
(507) 288-3890   Fax—(507) 252-1340

Nationally certified career counselor offers career assessment, testing and job-search coaching. Also provides job leads and workshops. Call for appointment and fees.

RESUME SPECIALISTS
& SERVICES

Probably no single component of the job hunting process gets more press and attention than the resume. And no wonder. Your resume can be a ticket—or roadblock—to your next job interview.

That's why so many job seekers turn to resume specialists. A good resume specialist can help you articulate your experience, responsibilities and skills. They will sum it up in a page or two which honestly represents your employment profile.

But judging who's a "good resume specialist" can be a tricky business.

Certainly you may be "good" enough to write your own resume, especially if you're a creative marketer and clear thinker with a firm grasp on your career experience. Or you can turn to Cousin Norm who wrote a "great" resume—and look at the job he just got.

Most career coaching services found in the previous sections list resume development in their palette of job-hunting services. But job hunters have yet another good option: Choosing from among the scores of resume specialists and services.

Don't look for career counseling or job-hunting advice at these specialized services. Resumes and related correspondence are generally their only business. That can be an advantage. A service that specializes in resumes must stay current on the newest looks, trends and technology to create resumes that get results.

Tips on working with Resume Specialists and Services

◆ Expect to find a significant variation in qualifications, services and fees among resume services. Some are staffed by professional writers. Others are primarily secretarial services. One individual may write your resume after an extensive interview. Others handle production and printing—no writing provided. Some shops do it all.

◆ If you elect to use a resume service, call several and screen them by phone. Inquire about the preparer's background or degree and experience preparing resumes for others in your field.

◆ Ask about fees upfront. Many preparers offer package prices; others charge by the hour. Don't necessarily select the cheapest service. Weigh price against quality and service. Fees usually start at $30. For that, a service will probably type your hand-written resume into a computer and hand over a master page that you can have printed elsewhere. Full packages (client interviews through printed resumes) generally start at $50-75 but can range upwards to $200 or more.

◆ Insist on seeing a portfolio of samples. Check out the individual's writing style, design selection, paper stock and printing quality.

◆ Even resumes are not immune from technology. Today, many employers, recruiters and placement services scan resumes into computer databases, then search them for keywords that match job qualifications. Scannable resumes require special preparation and attention. A good resume specialist will be on top of the trends.

◆ Determine whether the service is familiar with the resume formats common to your field or profession. If you're a senior systems analyst, think twice before you contract with a service that typically prepares artsy resumes for ad agency types.

A PLUS TYPING AND WORD PROCESSING

227 Central, Suite 107
Osseo, MN 55369
(612) 425-8878   Fax—(612) 425-8876

Services include resume writing, layout and cover letters. Also provides laser printing and disk storage. Call for appointment and fees. Free consultation.

ABILITY RESUME SERVICES

1111 W. 22nd St., Suite 109
Minneapolis, MN 55405
(612) 377-6939

Services include client consultation, writing, editing, layout and laser printing of resumes, cover letters, and reference sheets. Free disk storage. Fees vary by services required. Call for appointment.

ALDRICH RESUME SERVICE

4405 Aldrich Ave. So.
Minneapolis, MN 55409
(612) 825-8663   Fax—(612) 825-2443

Services include client consultation, resume writing, editing, layout, formatting, cover letters. Also provides computer-generated laser printing, disk storage and reference sheets. Free initial consultation. Call for appointment and fees.

BUSINESS OFFICE SUPPORT SERVICES

2499 Rice St., Suite 240
Roseville, MN 55113
(612) 490-0172   Fax—(612) 490-0581

Services include resume writing and editing, disk storage. Laser printouts available. Fees start at $45 for desktop publishing a one-page resume. Additional charges apply for consultation. Call for information.

CAREERSENSE

Victoria Crossing West, 867 Grand Avenue
St. Paul, MN 55105
(612) 222-4312
Fax—(612) 222-1317

Broad range of services include client consultation, resume writing, editing, layout, formatting, laser printouts and disk storage. Also develops cover letters. Additional services include career assessment, transition and outplacement counseling. Call for appointment. Fees: $40/hour; $70/basic package.

CORPORATE INFORMATION TECHNOLOGY SERVICES

2304 University Ave.
St. Paul, MN 55114
(612) 646-2476
Fax—(612) 646-4279

Free initial visit. Provides resume writing services, editing, layout and formatting. Also develops cover letters, job-search mailings. Laser printouts, disk storage, training on software packages. Call for appointment. Fees start at $20 per page.

FINE LINE RESUME SERVICE

3025 Harbor Lane, Suite 110B
Plymouth, MN 55447
(612) 553-9937
Fax—(612) 553-0077

Free initial consultation. Complete resume development services include client consultation, writing, editing, layout. Also prepares cover letters. Laser printing and disk storage available. Resume-writing fees start at $85. Call for appointment.

GISLESON WRITING SERVICES

2147 University Ave. W., Suite 218
St. Paul, MN 55114-1327
(612) 644-6408   Fax—(612) 645-3530

Internet address: http://calhoun.lakes.com/~gisleson
E-mail: gisleson@calhoun.lakes.com

Offers resume writing, editing, layout, laser printing (600 dpi laser printing). Cover letters, disk storage, applications and homepages. Fees start at $25 for typesetting and printing one-page resume. Hourly fees, $50. Call for an appointment. Weekday, weekend and evening hours.

INFORMATION MANAGEMENT SYSTEMS, INC.

2200 University Ave. W., Suite 130
St. Paul, MN 55114
(612) 642-2525   Fax—(612) 642-2520

Offers consultation, profile development and writing, printing, letters and support materials. Disk access and storage. Call for appointment and fees.

KATHLEEN BROGAN

Richfield, MN 55423
(612) 866-8940   Fax—(612) 869-2927

Offers writing, editing, layout, and formatting of resumes and job-search correspondence. Laser printouts and disk storage available. Free initial visit. Fees start at $50. Call for appointment.

OMNI / OFFICEPLUS

8400 Normandale Lake Blvd.
Bloomington, MN 55437
(612) 921-2300
Fax—(612) 921-2309
E-mail: tboling@OfficePlus.com

601 Lakeshore Pkwy.
Minnetonka, MN 55305
(612) 449-5100
Fax—(612) 449-5101

Resume writing/editing, layout, cover letters, laser printing, disk storage. Fees start at $25 for laser-printed one-page resume. Call for appointment.

PENCRAFT RESUME SERVICE

1020 E. 146th St., Suite 141
Burnsville, MN 55337
(612) 431-5962   Fax—(612) 891-4446

Resume development services include writing, editing, layout, cover letters, laser printing and disk storage. Computer-generated, laser-printed resumes start at $35. Package prices also available. Call for free consultation appointment.

PERSONAL PROFILE SERVICES

St. Paul, MN 55108
(612) 646-9636

Conducts in-depth, taped interview and provides resume and other related writing services. Also provides disk storage. Directed resumes and cover letters start at $75. Call to schedule an appointment.

PROFESSIONAL PROFILES

Lakeville, MN 55044
(612) 435-1952   Fax—(612) 435-6625

Services include client consultation, resume writing, layout, formatting, laser printouts and disk storage. Also prepares cover-letter correspondence. Free initial visit. Call for appointment. Package prices are available.

REFERENCE POINT

Coon Rapids, MN 55433
(612) 422-2021

Resume development services include consultation with client, resume writing, editing, formatting and disk storage. Also prepares cover letters and offers specialty stationery. Call for fee information or to schedule an appointment.

RESUME SPECIALISTS

3033 Excelsior Blvd., Suite 444
Minneapolis, MN 55416
(612) 928-0660   Fax—(612) 929-3045

Broad range of resume development services include resume writing, layout, cover letters, laser printing. Also offers resume seminars, job-search coaching and interview tips. Call for fee information or to schedule an appointment.

STANDBY SECRETARIES, INC.

2233 Hamline Ave., Suite 511
Roseville, MN 55113
(612) 636-2788   Fax—(612) 636-8799

Services include resume writing, layout, laser printing, disk storage. Also prepares cover letters. Fees start at $35 for word processed, two-page resume with laser printout.

THE RESUME PLACE

Plymouth, MN
(612) 559-4204
Fax—(612) 551-1932

Provides client consultation, resume writing and editing services, layout, laser printing and disk storage. Also prepares cover letters. Full-service resume package starts at $150.

THE RESUME SHOP

Stillwater, MN 55082
Phone/Fax—(612) 439-6903

Offers range of services including resume writing, layout, formatting, printouts and disk storage. Also produces cover letters, business portfolios, business cards and brochures. Hourly fees start at $20. Call for appointment.

GREATER MINNESOTA

ADMINISTRATIVE OFFICE SERVICES, INC.

400 E. St. Germain
St. Cloud, MN 56304
(320) 253-2532

Fees start at $30 for one-page resume. Guarantees delivery in 24 hours. After-hours and weekend services by appointment.

ADVANTAGE WORD PROCESSING

4945 Spirit Lake Road
Mountain Iron, MN 55768
(218) 735-8600

Provides client consultation, resume writing, editing, layout, formatting. Cover letters, thank you letters, laser printouts, disk storage and mock interviews. Call for appointment. Prices start at $15.

CAREER CONNECTIONS

P.O. Box 266
Albert Lea, MN 56007
(507) 373-1736
Internet address: http://deskmedia.com~ccent/cash.html
E-mail: ccent@deskmedia.com

Free initial consultation. Resume writing, layout, formatting, printouts. Cover letters, disk storage. Provides resume reference manual with initial deposit. Prices start at $45. Call for appointment.

CITY SECRETARY INC.

916 Broadway
Alexandria, MN 56308
(320) 763-5881   Fax—(320) 763-7862

Resume writing, formatting, cover letters, laser printouts. Copying/answering services, mailings, send/receive faxes. Call for appointment. Resume packages start at $18.50.

GREATER MINNESOTA

DESIGN RESUME & PAGE LAYOUT
Rochester, MN 55901
(507) 285-1657

Services include consultation with client, resume writing, layout, formatting, laser printouts and disk storage. Also prepares cover letters, and provides wallet-size networking cards. Free initial visit. Prices start at $25. Call for appointment.

DIANE'S SECRETARIAL SERVICE
102 First Street N.W.
Bemidji, MN 56601
(218) 751-7408

Provides resume writing, typing, formatting, printouts, cover letters, disk storage. Resume typing starts at $12. Other services offered at additional cost. Call for appointment.

ELECTRONIC INK
St. Cloud, MN 56301
(320) 253-0975
Fax—(320) 253-1790

Services include client consultation, resume writing, editing, layout, laser printing, disk storage. Also prepares cover letters. Call to schedule an appointment. Fees start at $85 for resume development and production.

EMPLOYMENT PLUS
920 W. Litchfield Ave.
Willmar, MN 56201
(320) 235-1707
Fax—(320) 235-8510

Services include resume writing, formatting, cover letters, laser printouts and disk storage. Basic resume package starts at $35. Call for appointment.

EXECUTIVE SUITES ON FIRST

2015 First St. So.
Willmar, MN 56201
(320) 235-9512   Fax—(320) 235-8633

Free initial visit. Resume writing, formatting, cover letters, laser printouts, disk storage. Call for information and fees.

JOBS UNLIMITED

1425 Paul Bunyon Drive N.W.
Bemidji, MN 56601
(218) 759-4835   Fax—(218) 759-4838

Services include client consultation, resume writing, editing, layout, formatting. Cover letters, laser printouts, disk storage. Free initial visit. Call for appointment.

KINETIC MEDIA INC.

P.O. Box 7151
Rochester, MN 55903
Phone/Fax—(507) 282-7787

Specializes in serving business and technical professionals. Client interview, resume writing, editing, formatting. Four-color self-promotion materials. Cover letters, disk storage. Interactive multimedia personal . marketing system. Call for appointment and pricing.

MAY WE HELP II

500 Folz Blvd., P.O. Box 310
Moose Lake, MN 55767
Phone/Fax—(218) 485-4123

Free initial visit. Resume writing, editing, formatting, printouts. Job applications, cover letters, disk storage. Also helps clients track job leads at no charge. Resumes start at $20. Call for appointment.

PERSONAL TOUCH OFFICE SERVICES

403 Division St.
Northfield, MN 55057
(507) 645-8811   Fax—(507) 645-9291

Client consultation, resume writing, layout, formatting, laser printouts.
Cover letters, disk storage. Free initial visit. Call for appointment and fees.

PETERSON TYPING SERVICE

Rochester, MN 55902
Phone/Fax—(507) 285-1350

Consultation interview, resume writing, editing, typing. Cover letters, laser
printing, disk storage. Free first visit. Packages start at $30.

PROFESSIONAL TYPING

St. Cloud, MN 56303
Phone/Fax—(320) 251-2741

Fees start at $20 to type and format a one-page resume. Also offers
typing service for cover letters and job-search correspondence.

TRI M GRAPHICS

625 E. Main St.
Owatonna, MN 55060
(507) 451-3920   Fax—(507) 451-7552

Provides cover letters, laser printouts, disk storage, resume typing,
formatting and resume printing. Prices start at $15 per page set-up.

WORD PROCESSING OF DULUTH

394 Lake Ave. So., Suite 303, Duluth, MN 55802
(218) 722-6911   Fax—(218) 722-0506

Client consultation, resume writing, editing, formatting, laser printouts,
disk storage, cover letters, job-search correspondence. Prepares reference
page, salary history charts. Basic package starts at $25.

SCHOOL-BASED
CAREER CENTERS

If you think schools are only good for earning degrees or diplomas, it's time to do your homework. Job seekers, career changers, students and alumni can be well served by organizations like these:

◆ Community and Technical Colleges

◆ Colleges and Universities

◆ High Schools and Local School Districts

School-based career centers are primarily in existence to help current or prospective students focus their career goals in order to map out an educational plan. They also assist graduates or alumni in the job-search process. Some centers are open to the public.

Career-related services generally include group or personalized career coaching, testing, assessments, resume assistance, placement services, access to the resource center or computerized career information. Many also provide job postings but most positions are geared to entry-level positions.

If you need basic warm-ups in job-search techniques or professional guidance in career decision-making, services available at school career centers can be valuable. And bargains too. Typically, services are free or modestly priced.

ANOKA-RAMSEY COMMUNITY COLLEGE
Career Center
11200 Mississippi Blvd. N.W.
Coon Rapids, MN 55433
(612) 422-3400   Fax—(612) 422-3341

Open to the public. Provides career assessment, individual counseling, resource center, classes, workshops. Call for information. Fees vary.

AUGSBURG COLLEGE
Career Services
2211 Riverside Avenue
Minneapolis, MN 55454
(612) 330-1162   Fax—(612) 330-1649

Open to current students and alumni. Provides individual career counseling, testing, job-search coaching, resource center. Free.

CENTURY COMMUNITY AND TECHNICAL COLLEGE
(Formerly N.E. Metro Technical & Lakewood Comm. Colleges)

3300 Century Ave. No.	3401 Century Avenue
White Bear Lake, MN 55110	White Bear Lake, MN 55110
(612) 770-2351	(612) 779-3370

Open to the public. Offers a range of career planning and job-search services. Call for information and fees.

COLLEGE OF ST. CATHERINE
Career Development
2004 Randolph Avenue
St. Paul, MN 55105
(612) 690-6510   Fax—(612) 690-6024

Open to current students and alumnae. Career planning, testing, job-search counseling, resource library, job leads. Free to students and alumnae for limited time; thereafter, $25 per hour for individual counseling.

DAKOTA COUNTY TECHNICAL COLLEGE
Career Assessment Center
1300 E. 145th Street
Rosemount, MN 55068
(612) 423-8409   Fax—(612) 423-7028

Open to the public. Offers career assessment, testing, individual/group counseling, job-search coaching. Also provides job leads, resource library, workshops, support group. Call for appointment. Use of resource center is free. Additional fees apply for testing, classes and workshops.

HAMLINE UNIVERSITY
Career Development Center
1536 Hewitt Avenue
St. Paul, MN 55104
(612) 641-2302   Fax—(612) 659-3085
Internet address: http://www.hamline.edu
E-mail: career@seq.hamline.edu

Open and free to students and alumni for two years following graduation. Alumni are served on space-available basis. Offers career planning, job-search counseling, resume development, resource library, workshops, job leads. Call for appointment and fees.

HENNEPIN TECHNICAL COLLEGE
Counseling Services

BROOKLYN PARK	EDEN PRAIRIE
9000 Brooklyn Blvd.	9200 Flying Cloud Drive
Brooklyn Park, MN 55445	Eden Prairie, MN 55347
(612) 425-3800	(612) 944-2222
Fax—(612) 550-2119	

Open to the public. Offers career and vocational counseling, financial aid counseling, testing and assessment. Open weekdays and evenings. Call for appointment or drop in.

HOPKINS HIGH SCHOOL ADULT CAREER CENTER
Hopkins Area Family Resource Center
915 Mainstreet
Hopkins, MN 55343
(612) 988-5350   Fax—(612) 988-5358

Open to adults on Wednesday evenings from 6:45-9:15 p.m. from September through May. Low-cost career assessment tests and interpretation ranging from $5-$25. Computerized vocational data bank, resource library. Drop in or call. Consultation staff on duty. Free.

LIFEWORKS
Bloomington Education Center

8900 Portland Ave. So.
Bloomington, MN 55420
(612) 885-8553
Fax—(612) 885-8640

5701 Normandale Road
Room 333
Edina, MN 55424
(612) 928-2579

Open to the public. Targeted to unemployed or underemployed individuals seeking improved positions. Offers individualized career planning and development, workshops, computerized career information, skills for getting and keeping a job, resource library and mobile job bank. Some training and internships available for eligible participants. Call for appointment. Free service.

MACALESTER COLLEGE
Career Development Center
1600 Grand Avenue
St. Paul, MN 55105
(612) 696-6384   Fax—(612) 696-6131

Open to current students and alumni. Individual career counseling, testing, resume development, resource library, internships, computerized job-seeking skills program, job postings. Call or write for appointment. No charge to students or alumni for one year after graduation.

TWIN CITIES

METROPOLITAN STATE UNIVERSITY
Resource Center

730 Hennepin Avenue
Minneapolis, MN 55403
(612) 373-2707

700 E. 7th Street
St. Paul, MN 55106
(612) 772-7647

Internet address: http://www.metro.msus.edu

Open to applicants, current students and graduates. Services include career testing, personal career counseling, computer-assisted resources. Call for appointment. Services are free; fees for interest testing.

MINNEAPOLIS COMMUNITY COLLEGE CAREER CENTER

1501 Hennepin Avenue
Minneapolis, MN 55403-1779
(612) 341-7040   Fax—(612) 341-7075

Services are open to the public. Computerized career exploration program. Also offers career exploration classes at a fee. Call for appointment.

MINNETONKA HIGH SCHOOL ADULT CAREER CENTER

18301 Highway 7
Minnetonka, MN 55345
(612) 470-3450   Fax—(612) 470-3785

For adults in career transition. Open to the public on drop-in basis most Mondays, 7-9 p.m. during school year. Interest and career testing, job-search assistance. Computerized career data. Free except for test scoring.

NORMANDALE COMMUNITY COLLEGE RESOURCE CENTER

9700 France Ave. So.
Bloomington, MN 55431
(612) 832-6350   Fax—(612) 832-6571

Open to the public. Provides individual and group career assessment and testing, workshops, job-search coaching. Fees range from $8-$70. No charge to access career resource center, software and Job Service Job Bank.

NORTH HENNEPIN COMMUNITY COLLEGE
Career Center
7411 85th Ave. No.
Brooklyn Park, MN 55445
(612) 424-0703   Fax—(612) 424-0929

Open to the public but targeted to students or prospective students. Services include use of interactive computer program for self-assessment and career information, access to Job Service Job Bank and resource library. Call for appointment. Free.

ROSEVILLE ADULT HIGH SCHOOL CAREER SERVICES
Fairview Community Center, 1910 W. County. Rd. B
Roseville, MN 55113
(612) 604-3553   Fax—(612) 604-3501

Open to the public. Offers career assessment, vocational testing, resource library, job-search coaching, computer resources. Free.

ST. LOUIS PARK DIST. 283 ADULT CAREER CENTER
6425 West 33rd Street
St. Louis Park, MN 55426
(612) 928-6133   Fax—(612) 928-6020

Open to the public but targeted to St. Louis Park residents. Provides career assessment, testing, workshops, job bank, resource library, resume preparation, job-search coaching, job leads. Call for appointment. Free.

ST. PAUL TECHNICAL COLLEGE
Student Services Career Center
235 Marshall Avenue
St. Paul, MN 55102
(612) 221-1370   Fax—(612) 221-1416

Open to the public. Provides career assessment, videotapes and computer programs for career exploration. Job placement assistance from staff and State Job Service representative. Free. Drop in.

UNIVERSITY OF MINNESOTA
Carlson School of Management
CAREER SERVICES CENTER
190 Humphrey Center, 271 19th Ave. So.
Minneapolis, MN 55455
(612) 624-0011   Fax—(612) 626-1822

Open to Carlson School of Management students and alumni. Offers career planning, job-search coaching, resource library, seminars, job leads, job fairs, internships, resume referral service. Call for appointment. Free to current students; $40/6 months for alumni.

UNIVERSITY OF MINNESOTA
College of Agriculture, Food, and Environmental Sciences
CAREER SERVICES OFFICE
272 Coffey Hall, 1420 Eckles Avenue
St. Paul, MN 55108
(612) 624-2710   Fax—(612) 625-1260

Open to U of M students and alumni. Services include individualized counseling, resume preparation, networking opportunities, resource materials, job leads, career fair. Call for appointment. Free.

UNIVERSITY OF MINNESOTA
College of Biological Sciences
CAREER INFORMATION CENTER
217 Snyder Hall, 1475 Gortner Avenue
St. Paul, MN 55108
(612) 624-9270   Fax—(612) 624-2785
Internet address: http://www.cbs.umn.edu/

Open to individuals interested in biology careers. Offers workshops, resume-writing assistance, resource library, employer information. Resume referral service for current students and alumni. Drop in. Free.

UNIVERSITY OF MINNESOTA
College of Education and Human Development

STUDENT AND PROFESSIONAL SERVICES
110 Wulling Hall
Minneapolis, MN 55455
(612) 625-6501   Fax—(612) 626-1580

Open to individuals interested in education careers. Provides career planning, job-search counseling, resume preparation, resource library, workshops, job leads, international teaching opportunities. Call for appointment. Most services are free.

UNIVERSITY OF MINNESOTA
College of Human Ecology

CAREER SERVICES CENTER
68 McNeal Hall, 1985 Buford Avenue
St. Paul, MN 55108
(612) 624-6762   Fax—(612) 625-7234

Free to CHE students and alumni. Offers career planning, job-search counseling, resume development, resource library, seminars and job leads. Call for appointment.

UNIVERSITY OF MINNESOTA
College of Liberal Arts

CAREER SERVICES
345 Fraser Hall, 106 Pleasant Street
Minneapolis, MN 55455
(612) 624-7505   Fax—(612) 624-2538

Open to CLA students and alumni. Services include internship and career planning assistance, resume and job-search help, career resource library. Also offers seminars and job postings. Call or drop in. Free to students and alumni for one year following graduation.

UNIVERSITY OF MINNESOTA
Dept. of Counseling, Continuing Education & Extension / University College (CEE/UC)

314 Nolte Center, 315 Pillsbury Drive S.E.
Minneapolis, MN 55455
(612) 625-2500   Fax—(612) 625-5364
E-mail: CEEADV@mail.cee.umn.edu

Open to individuals considering further education at the University through CEE/UC. Offers career counseling, testing, workshops. Call for information and fees.

UNIVERSITY OF MINNESOTA
Hubert H. Humphrey Institute of Public Affairs

OFFICE OF CAREER SERVICES
301 19th Ave. So.
Minneapolis, MN 55455
(612) 625-2847   Fax—(612) 625-6351

Open only to Humphrey students and alumni. Assistance with career planning, job-search skills, resume development, resource materials, job leads. Call for appointment. Free.

UNIVERSITY OF MINNESOTA
Institute of Technology

CAREER SERVICES
50 Lind Hall, 207 Church St. S.E.
Minneapolis, MN 55455
(612) 624-4090   Fax—(612) 626-0261

Open to current students and alumni. Provides a variety of services including career planning, job-search and resume assistance. Also offers resource library, seminars, current job openings and resume referral service. Call for appointment.

UNIVERSITY OF MINNESOTA
University Counseling and Consulting Services
109 Eddy Hall, 192 Pillsbury Drive S.E.
Minneapolis, MN 55455
(612) 624-8344   Fax—(612) 624-0207

Primarily open and free to prospective and current students. Non-students served on availability basis. Career assessment, testing, individual/group career counseling, resource center, workshops. Call for information, fees.

UNIVERSITY OF MINNESOTA
Vocational Assessment Clinic
N555 Elliott Hall, 75 East River Road
Minneapolis, MN 55455
(612) 625-1519   Fax—(612) 626-2079

Open to adults who are not full-time students at the University of Minnesota. Offers vocational assessment, career planning, individual counseling. Call for appointment. Individual counseling fees, $225-$250.

UNIVERSITY OF ST. THOMAS
Counseling and Career Services
350 Murray-Herrick, 2115 Summit Avenue
St. Paul, MN 55105
(612) 962-6761   Fax—(612) 962-6775

Open to current students and alumni. Provides career planning, resume preparation, job-search coaching, resource library, interest/career testing, job leads. Call for appointment. Free for one year after graduation.

WESTONKA COMMUNITY ACTION NETWORK
5600 Lynwood Blvd., Mound, MN 55364
(612) 472-0742

Open to residents of Hennepin County. Offers career assessment and testing, job bank, resource library, resume preparation, job-search coaching and job leads. Call for appointment. Free.

ALEXANDRIA TECHNICAL COLLEGE
Career Planning and Assessment Center
1601 Jefferson
Alexandria, MN 56308
(320) 762-0221   (800) 253-9884   Fax—(320) 762-4501

Open to the public but targeted to students. Services include career assessment and testing, job placement assistance and career resource library. Also offers job-search coaching and retraining. Call for appointment. Free.

AUSTIN COMMUNITY COLLEGE
Counseling and Career Center
1600 8th Ave. N.W.
Austin, MN 55912
(507) 433-0505   Fax—(507) 433-0515

Open to the public. Services include career assessment and testing, workshops, job bank and resource library. Call for appointment. Free, but fees are charged for some tests.

BEMIDJI STATE UNIVERSITY
Career Services
1500 Birchmont Drive N.E.
Bemidji, MN 56601-2669
(218) 755-2038   Fax—(218) 755-4115
E-mail: MrThomas@vax1.Bemidji.msus.edu

Open to current or prospective students and alumni. Services include career assessment, job-search coaching, resume assistance, job placement, career resource library, credential services. Also provides job vacancy bulletins and job fairs. Call or drop in for services. Fees apply for some services.

CENTRAL LAKES COLLEGE
Community College Campus Career Center
501 W. College Drive
Brainerd, MN 56401
(218) 828-2525　(800) 933-0346　Fax—(218) 828-2710

Open to the public but targeted to students. Provides career assessment, testing, resource library, job-search coaching, career planning classes, job leads. Also offers vocational information. Call for appointment. Free.

CENTRAL LAKES COLLEGE
Staples Technical College Career Placement
1830 Airport Road
Staples, MN 56479
(218) 894-1168　Fax—(218) 894-2546

Open to the public. Offers career assessment, testing, workshops, resource library, job-search coaching, job leads. Call for appointment. Free.

COLLEGE OF ST. BENEDICT CAREER SERVICES
37 So. College Avenue
St. Joseph, MN 56374
(320) 363-5707　Fax—(320) 363-5600

Open only to current students and alumni. Offers career and job-search counseling, interest/personality testing, computer-based inventories. Publishes job vacancy bulletin. Call for appointment and fees.

COLLEGE OF ST. SCHOLASTICA
Student Development Center
1200 Kenwood
Duluth, MN 55811
(218) 723-6085　Fax—(218) 723-6482

Open only to enrolled students and alumni. Offers career counseling and testing, job-search coaching, resource library, job bank, career classes, credential maintenance and mailing. Call for appointment. Free.

GREATER MINNESOTA

FARIBAULT SENIOR HIGH SCHOOL
Career Resource Center
330 9th Ave. S.W.
Faribault, MN 55021
(507) 334-5527

Open to the public. Services include career assessment, vocational testing, job-search coaching and career resource library. Call for appointment. Free.

FERGUS FALLS COMMUNITY COLLEGE
Career Information Center
1414 College Way
Fergus Falls, MN 56537
(218) 739-7555
Fax—(218) 739-7475

Open to the public. Services include career assessment and testing, job-search workshops, job-search coaching. Also provides access to computerized career information and a resource library. Free for students; $5 one-time fee to residents.

FOND DU LAC COMMUNITY COLLEGE
College Center
2101 14th Street
Cloquet, MN 55720
(218) 879-0800   Fax—(218) 879-0814

Internet address: http://www.fdl.cc.mn.us//
E-mail: dklocke@mail.fdl.cc.mn.us

Open to the public but targeted to enrolled students. Services include career assessment, resource library, resume and interview assistance. Also provides career exploration and job-search classes. Call for appointment and fee information.

GREATER MINNESOTA

HASTINGS SENIOR HIGH SCHOOL
Career Resource Center
1000 11th St. W.
Hastings, MN 55033-2597
(612) 438-0753   Fax—(612) 437-7332

Open to the public, weekdays, throughout school year. Offers career resource library with computerized career information, vocational and college catalogs, career publications. Call for appointment. Free.

HIBBING COMMUNITY COLLEGE
Career Center
1515 E. 25th Street
Hibbing, MN 55746
(218) 262-6700   Fax—(218) 262-6717

Open to the public but targeted to enrolled students. Services include career assessment, testing, vocational software, resource library. Call for appointment. Free or low-cost.

ITASCA COMMUNITY COLLEGE
1851 E. Hwy. 169
Grand Rapids, MN 55744
(218) 327-4460   (800) 996-6422   Fax—(218) 327-4350

Open to the public but targeted to current students. Offers career testing, resource library. Call for an appointment. Free.

LAKE SUPERIOR COLLEGE
Career Center
2101 Trinity Road
Duluth, MN 55811
(218) 722-2801   Fax—(218) 722-2899

Open to the public. Offers career assessment and testing, workshops, resource library, job placement (for grads only), women's resource center. Call for an appointment. Free.

GREATER MINNESOTA

MINNESOTA RIVERLAND TECHNICAL COLLEGE

REACH CENTER
1926 College View Road S.E.
Rochester, MN 55904
(507) 280-3120
(800) 247-1296

CAREER CENTER
1900 N.W. 8th Avenue
Austin, MN 55912
(507) 433-0600   (800) 247-5039
Fax—(507) 433-0665
E-mail: mbush@rtc.tec.mn.us

CAREER RESOURCE CENTER
1225 S.W. Third Street
Faribault, MN 55021
(507) 334-3965   Fax—(507) 332-5888

Open to the public during school year. Services vary by location but may include career assessment, testing, job-search coaching, workshops, resource library. Also coaches single parents, displaced homemakers and individuals pursuing non-traditional careers. Call for appointment. Free.

NORTHWEST TECHNICAL COLLEGE
Employment Services

Call for locations in Bemidji, Detroit Lakes, E. Grand Forks, Moorhead, Wadena

(218) 631-3530   (800) 247-2007 ext. 270   Fax—(218) 631-9207
E-mail: vicki@adm.wadena.tec.mn.us

Open only to students and graduates. Offers career assessment, job-search assistance and resource library, workshops, job placement, computerized career information. Call for appointment. Free.

PINE TECHNICAL COLLEGE
1000 Fourth Street
Pine City, MN 55063
(320) 629-6764   (800) 521-7463   Fax—(320) 629-7603

Open to the public. Career assessment, job placement, workshops, resource library, job-search coaching. Access to Job Service Job Bank and Minnesota Career Information System. Call for an appointment. Free.

RAINY RIVER COMMUNITY COLLEGE
Career Center
1501 Highway 71
International Falls, MN 56649
(218) 285-7722   Fax—(218) 285-2239
TDD—(218) 285-2261

Open to the public but services are primarily targeted to enrolled students. Center offers career assessment, testing, resume and interviewing assistance, workshops, career development classes. Also offers access to career resource library. Call for appointment. Fees for courses and workshops.

RANGE TECHNICAL COLLEGE

EVELETH CAMPUS
1100 Industrial Park Dr.
Eveleth, MN 55734
(218) 744-3302
(800) 345-2884
Fax—(218) 744-3486

HIBBING CAMPUS
2900 E. Beltline
Hibbing, MN 55746
(218) 262-7200
(800) 433-9989

Open to the public. Services include career assessment and testing, workshops, job placement, resource library, job-search coaching, job leads, supplemental services, tutoring, minority vocational advising. Call for appointment and fees.

ROCHESTER COMMUNITY COLLEGE
Counseling Center
851 30th Ave. S.E.
Rochester, MN 55904
(507) 285-7260   Fax—(507) 285-7496

Career assessment, testing, job-search coaching and workshops are free and available to current students only. The resource library is open to the public. Call for appointment.

ST. CLOUD STATE UNIVERSITY
Career Services

AS-101, 720 So. Fourth Avenue

St. Cloud, MN 56301

(320) 255-2151   Fax—(320) 654-5167

Internet address:

http://condor.stcloud.msus.edu/"careersv/index.html

E-mail: rmurray@tigger.stcloud.msus.edu

Open to the public. Assistance with resumes, interviewing and job-search skills. Offers resource library with computer database indexing job opportunities across the country. Job vacancy bulletin. Call for appointment. Free.

ST. CLOUD TECHNICAL COLLEGE
Placement Office

1540 Northway Drive

St. Cloud, MN 56303

(320) 654-5000   (800) 222-1009   Fax—(320) 654-5981

E-mail: tlg@cloud.tec.mn.us

Open only to current students and alumni. Services include career planning, job-search counseling, resume development. Also provides assistance with networking, interviewing, negotiating skills. Resource library, job leads and annual job fair. Call for appointment. Free.

ST. JOHN'S UNIVERSITY
Counseling and Career Services

Collegeville, MN 56321-2000

(320) 363-3791   Fax—(320) 363-2504

Open only to current students and alumni. Services include career counseling, interest assessment. Also provides access to Internet, resource library and corporate information databases. Call for appointment and fees.

ST. OLAF COLLEGE
Career Development Center
1520 St. Olaf Avenue
Northfield, MN 55057
(507) 646-3268

Open only to current students and alumni. Provides career assessment, testing, job-search coaching, job leads, internship opportunities, resource library. Call for appointment.

SOUTH CENTRAL TECHNICAL COLLEGE

LIBRARY RESOURCE CENTER	PLACEMENT OFFICE
2200 Tech Drive	1920 Lee Blvd.
Albert Lea, MN 56007	North Mankato, MN 56002
(507) 373-0656	(507) 389-7225
(800) 333-2584	(800) 722-9359
Fax—(507) 373-1758	

Open to the public but targeted to students. Offers career assessment, testing, job-search coaching and access to job leads through the Minnesota Job Service Job Bank. Drop in. Free.

SOUTHWEST STATE UNIVERSITY
Career Services
Bellows 268, 1501 State Street
Marshall, MN 56258
(507) 537-6221
Fax—(507) 537-7154
E-mail: 553cwm@rickyvs.southwest.msus.edu

Open to the public. Services include career assessment, vocational testing, job-search coaching, resume and interview preparation and assistance with job placement. Also offers job-search workshops and resource library. Drop in. Free.

GREATER MINNESOTA

SOUTHWESTERN TECHNICAL COLLEGE
Career Centers

1011 First St. W.
Canby, MN 56220
(612) 223-7252
(800) 658-2535

1593 11th Ave.
Granite Falls, MN 56241
(320) 564-4511
(800) 657-3247

401 W. Street
Jackson, MN 56143
(507) 847-3320
(800) 658-2522

1314 No. Hiawatha
Pipestone, MN 56164
(507) 825-5471   (800) 658-2330
Fax—(507) 825-4656

Open to the public. Career services vary by location but generally include career assessment, testing, job leads, job-search coaching and assistance with resume and interview preparation. Most locations also offer access to a career resource library. Call for information or to schedule an appointment. Free.

UNIVERSITY OF MINNESOTA—CROOKSTON
Counseling and Career Center
Bede Hall, Room 106
Crookston, MN 56716
(218) 281-8585 or (218) 281-8586
Fax—(218) 281-8584

Internet address: http://www.umn.edu/
E-mail: Cavalier@mail.crk.umn.edu

Career services are open to the public but targeted to enrolled students and graduates. The career center offers a broad selection of services including career assessment and testing, job-search coaching, job leads, assistance with resume and interview preparation. Services also include access to the resource library. Call for an appointment or drop in. Fees start at $20.

UNIVERSITY OF MINNESOTA—DULUTH
Career Services

21 Campus Center, 10 University Dr.
Duluth, MN 55812
(218) 726-7985   Fax—(218) 726-6394

Internet address: http://www.d.umn.edu
E-mail: carserv@ub.d.umn.edu

Open only to UMD students. Offers career assessment, testing, job-search coaching, resume assistance, workshops, job placement, resource library. Call for appointment. Fees for testing, placement credentials, job-vacancy bulletin.

WINONA STATE UNIVERSITY
Career Planning and Placement

110 Gildemeister Hall
Winona, MN 55987
(507) 457-5340   Fax—(507) 457-5516

Open to WSU students and alumni. Services include job-search coaching, job leads, resource library, job fairs. Call for appointment. Alumni fees, $25 per year.

WINONA TECHNICAL COLLEGE
Student Services Center

P.O. Box 409, 1250 Homer Road
Winona, MN 55987
(507) 454-4600   (800) 372-8164   Fax—(507) 452-1564

Open to the public. Assists with career assessment and job-search skills. Also offers testing, job leads and placement, resource library. Call for an appointment. Free.

2

FOR
ONLINE &
MULTIMEDIA
JOB SEEKING

◆ Internet Employment Resources

◆ Multimedia Career Products

◆ Library & Online Resources

Welcome to the Electronic Age of Job Seeking. Now, with the help of a few microprocessors and silicon chips, you can boldly go where no job seeker has gone before.

This chapter is designed to introduce you to a high-powered collection of electronic resources that can charge up your job hunt. To borrow from the title of a popular guide by Joyce Lain Kennedy: *Hook Up. Get Hired!*

In the following sections, we have highlighted several promising types of multimedia and online resources. For cybernaut job seekers, our list of career-track Internet sites will speed them to vast databases of information about jobs, careers, industries and employers.
For those who own, or have access to a personal computer, an interesting selection of software may offer computerized solutions to the daunting tasks of focusing a job hunt and staying on track. Multimedia career resources—videos, audio cassettes, broadcast and CD-ROMs—provide an entertaining twist to plain-vanilla job-search instruction. And a variety of public and school career libraries offer job seekers a wealth of high- and low-tech research options.

INTERNET EMPLOYMENT

RESOURCES

The Internet, with its sizzle and promise is the new frontier for job seekers. Today, with access to the Internet, you can transform your personal computer into a powerful job-search command center. Here's how:

With the touch of a keystroke, now you can browse through vast databases of job openings. Publish your resume online. Electronically apply for a job. Research prospective employers and industry trends. Network online with other job seekers or peers in your field. Download pre-designed resume templates. Gather expert job-search tips. Work on career-assessment exercises. You can even access online career coaching.

A cyberspace job search can do all these things and more—but don't over-estimate the results. Like any new frontier, online job seeking is a wild uncharted territory. No one can testify to its actual effectiveness in helping *real people find real jobs.*

Just because you can post a resume on a global billboard, will your resume stand out from among a crowd of thousands? Just because you can browse through worldwide job postings, will more jobs suddenly appear in areas or industries where opportunities are few? And, will anything ever replace the value of good old-fashioned people-to-people networking?

Internet job resources are one tool in a field of many that may lead you to your next job. Keep it in perspective. Happy hunting.

TIPS FOR YOUR INTERNET JOB SEARCH

◆ This is NOT a beginner's guide to the Internet. If you are new to online services, enroll in a class through community education or your local public library. Many guidebooks also provide a valuable introduction to the Internet. Check your library or bookstore for titles.

◆ Some books focus exclusively on the Internet job search. Consider these: **Hook Up, Get Hired** and **Electronic Job Search Revolution,** both by J. L. Kennedy (John Wiley & Sons), **The Online Job Search Companion** by J. C. Gonyea (McGraw-Hill) and **Be Your Own Headhunter Online** by P. Dixon and S. Tiersten (Random House).

◆ To access the Internet, you need a computer, modem (min. 14,400 baud is recommended), an account with a commercial online service or local Internet provider and special software. Access charges vary, so shop around. In some areas, you may also pay long-distance connect charges.

◆ The World Wide Web is a fascinating way to browse the Internet. Web sites offer snappy graphics and click-of-the-mouse links to related sites. To access the Web you need software such as Netscape or Mosaic.

◆ To get to a Web site, you must know the Uniform Resource Locator ("URL"), a series of letters and numbers that act as the address. Copy URLS exactly as noted. Do not add spaces if none are designated.

◆ If you don't own a computer or can't afford Internet access, call your local library, school district, college career center or Job Service office. They may provide free access or make referrals to other sources. Two Twin Cities coffee houses offer fee-paid access to the Internet: **CyberX** at 3001 Lyndale So., Mpls., (612) 824-3558; and **Cahoots Coffee Bar** at 1562 Selby Ave., St. Paul, (612) 644-6778.

◆ Internet navigational aids let you search the net for topics of interest. Start your search at one or more of these popular sites:

COMPREHENSIVE LIST OF SITES
http://www.netgen.com/cgi/comprehensive

LYCOS SEARCH
http://lycos-tmp1.psc.edu/cgi-bin/flpursuit?

THE WHOLE INTERNET CATALOG
http://www-e1c.gnn.com/gnn/wic/

WEBCRAWLER
http://webcrawler.com/WebCrawler/WebQuery.html

WWW YELLOW PAGES
http://www.cba.uh.edu/ylowpges/ylowpges.html

YAHOO
http://www.yahoo.com

◆ While cruising the Internet, be prepared for time-consuming jumps to new locations, deadends, overlap—and unexpected surprises. You may also encounter notices like, "Connection Refused By Host." This may mean that the site has changed location. Try using a navigational tool to track down the new address. The message may also mean that the site is popular and, at that moment, the computer won't let you in. Keep trying. You may ultimately connect.

◆ Bulletin Board Systems (BBS) are computers you can tap into without Internet access. Keep in mind you will pay long-distance charges to access servers outside of your local calling area. There are thousands of active bulletin boards and hundreds for job seekers. We have not included BBS listings in this section. For a good list, check out the **Mother of All BBS** at http://wwwmbb.cs.colorado.edu/mbb

The listings below are a sampling of interesting career-related Internet sites. Other online resources are included in the Minnesota Job Seeker's Sourcebook *in chapter leads and organizational listings.*

ADAMS JOBBANK ONLINE

http://www.adamsonline.com/

Job listings, online career publications, advice from career experts, resume uploads, interview strategies, company profiles.

AMERICA'S EMPLOYERS

http://www.americasemployers.com/

Database of employers, job-search tips, recruiters by specialty, positions available, resume bank, entrepreneurial options, electronic networking.

AMERICA'S JOB BANK

U.S. Department of Labor and State Public Employment Agency

http://www.ajb.dni.us/index.html

Links to state-run job banks and services.

BRAVE NEW WORK WORLD

http://www.newwork.com

Career-related resources, articles and book reviews.

CAREER CHOICES

http://www.umanitoba.ca/counselling/careers.html

Links to information and resources about a variety of careers.

CAREER DEVELOPMENT MANUAL

http://www.adm.uwaterloo.ca/infocecs/CRC/manual-home.html

Online self-assessment exercises, resources for researching prospective employers, job-search tips, worksheets to organize your job search.

CAREER MOSAIC

http://www.service.com/cm/cm1.html

High-tech employers, searchable index of jobs posted to 20+ newsgroups.

CAREER PLANNING PROCESS

http://www.cba.bgsu.edu/class/webclass/nagye/career/process.html

Online career assessment exercises.

CAREER & RESUME MANAGEMENT FOR THE 21ST CENTURY

http://crm21.com

Online articles, job listings, fee-based resume uploads, resources for women.

CAREER SHOP

http://www.tenkey.com/cshop/

Online database of resumes and nationwide job postings.

CAREERNET

http://www.careers.org/

Over 1,300 links to regional and national employment resources.

CAREERSITE

http://www.careersite.com/

Online database of resumes and nationwide job postings.

CAREERWEB

http://www.cweb.com

Job listings, career-readiness inventory, online career resources, bookstore.

CAREERS ON-LINE

http://www.disserv.stu.umn.edu/TC/Grants/COL/

Minnesota job postings and information for people with disabilities.

COLLEGE GRAD JOB HUNTER

http://www.execpc.com/~insider/

Online job listings and resume postings, job tips and links to career sites.

COMMERCIAL ONLINE SERVICES

AMERICA ONLINE
(800) 827-6364

MICROSOFT NETWORK
(800) 386-5550

COMPUSERVE
(800) 848-8199

PRODIGY
(800) 776-3449

Commercial online services offer a variety of career centers and services ranging from simple to sophisticated. Call for membership details.

COMPUTERWORLD'S CENTER FOR PROFESSIONAL DEVELOPMENT

http://careers.computerworld.com

Job listings, employer profiles, career events, educational resources.

CONTRACT EMPLOYMENT WEEKLY

http://www.ceweekly.wa.com/

Nationwide job listings for contract technical positions.

EMPLOYMENT OPPORTUNITIES & JOB RESOURCES ON THE INTERNET

http://www.wpi.edu/~mfriley/jobguide.html

Extensive links to Internet job-search and related resources.

E-SPAN INTERACTIVE EMPLOYMENT NETWORK

http://www.espan.com/

Nationwide job bank, resumes, articles, employer profiles, salary guides.

FEDERAL JOBS DATABASE

http://www.jobweb.org/fedjobsr.htm

Searchable nationwide job listings with federal government.

FRS FEDERAL JOBS CENTRAL

http://www.fedjobs.com

Fee-based job matching service, career tips and publications.

H.E.A.R.T. / CAREER CONNECTIONS

http://www.career.com/

Job listings and resume builder.

HELP WANTED USA

http://iccweb.com/employ1.html

Nationwide job postings for professional positions.

HOOVER'S ONLINE

http://www.hoovers.com/

Company profiles, business news and directory of corporate Web sites.

I.O.M.A.

http://ioma.com/ioma/

Excellent jump point to locate online research resources related to business and many fields and industries.

INTELLIMATCH ON-LINE CAREER SERVICES

http://www.intellimatch.com/

Ability to complete and post a structured online resume.

INTERNATIONAL JOB SEARCH RESOURCES

http://hosea.atc.ll.mit.edu:8000/jobs.html

Links to international job sources: employers, job databases and recruiters.

INTERNET CAREER CONNECTION

http://iccweb.com

Nationwide job openings, resume database, career library and products.

INTERNET JOB SURFER

http://www.rpi.edu/dept/cdc/jobsurfer.html

Links to job databases and resume banks, services for human resources.

JOB HUNT

http://rescomp.stanford.edu/jobs.html

Guide to online employment resources and services.

JOB SEARCH AND EMPLOYMENT OPPORTUNITIES: BEST BETS FROM THE NET

http://www.lib.umich.edu/chdocs/employment/

Extensive guide to online employment resources and services.

JOB TRAK

http://www.jobtrak.com

Job listings, company profiles, career tips, guide to graduate schools.

JOBCENTER EMPLOYMENT SERVICES

http://www.jobcenter.com/

Career articles, fee-based resume uploads and job matching service.

JOBS!

http://copper.ucs.indiana.edu/~dvasilef/jobsearch.html

Index of companies, nationwide, that post online job listings.

JOBTAILOR

http://www.jobtailor.com/

Free resume uploads and ability to respond to nationwide job postings.

JOBWEB

http://www.jobweb.org

Career resources, job fairs, company profiles and federal jobs database.

MEDSEARCH™ AMERICA

http://www.medsearch.com

Nationwide healthcare job listings, employer and recruiter profiles, resume postings and electronic networking forums.

MINNESOTA CAREER STORE

Resource Publishing Group Inc.

http://www.careerstore.com

Minnesota career resources, job-search tips, online sampler edition of the Twin Cities Job Seeker's Calendar. Links to related online career sites.

MINNESOTA-AREA EMPLOYERS

http://disserv.stu.umn.edu/mnemp/

Small but growing list of Minnesota employers that post jobs online.

MINNESOTA WWW SITES

http://www.mr.net/minnesota/

Links to Minnesota Web sites including companies, schools, Internet access providers, media, associations and more.

MINNESOTA DEPARTMENT OF ECONOMIC SECURITY

http://mn.jobsearch.org/ajb/mn.htm

Searchable database of Minnesota jobs, labor market information, job tips.

MN.JOBS

news:mn.jobs

Newsgroup with job postings for Minnesota positions, mostly technical.

MONSTER BOARD

http://199.94.216.72:80/home.html

Employer profiles, career tips, resume uploads, job postings, career events.

NATIONJOB NETWORK™

http://www.nationjob.com/

Database of nationwide job postings and employer profiles.

NCS CAREER MAGAZINE

http://plaza.xor.com/careermag/

Job and resume postings, employer profiles, online career publications.

NERD WORLD: JOBS

http://challenge.tiac.net/users/dstein/nw102.html

Extensive index and links to career-related Web sites.

NETWORKING ON THE NETWORK

http://www.wm.edu/catapult/pagre-n.html

Tips on how to use the Internet for effective networking.

OCCUPATIONAL OUTLOOK HANDBOOK

http://stats.bls.gov:80/ocohome.htm

Occupational information and projections. Links to BLS employment data.

ONLINE CAREER CENTER

http://www.occ.com/occ/HomePage.html

Online job bank, resume referral service and career tips.

ONLINE EMPLOYMENT LISTING SERVICE FOR MINNESOTA

http://www.e-zone.com/employment/index.html#top

Minnesota job postings and resume uploads for technical positions.

PIONEER PLANET

http://www.pioneerplanet.com/index.htm

Online edition of the St. Paul Pioneer Press. News briefs and searchable classified ads including employment listings.

QUICK GUIDE TO RESUME WRITING

http://www.jobweb.org/catapult/guenov/sampleres.html

Resume tips, resume action words, key competencies desired by employers.

SOFTWARE JOBS HOME PAGE

http://clever.net/swjobs

News and job postings for software engineers and database professionals.

STAR TRIBUNE ONLINE / WEB EDITION

http://www.startribune.com/

News summaries and online classified ads including employment.

THE CATAPAULT

http://www.jobweb.org/catapult/catapult.htm

Links to nationwide career sites. Employment resources organized by field.

TWIN CITIES JOBS PAGE

http://fentonnet.com/jobs.html

Resume uploads and limited number of local job postings.

UNIVERSITY OF MINNESOTA JOB POSTINGS

http://www.umn.edu/hrdept/jobs/

Academic and civil service full- and part-time positions.

VIRTUAL JOB FAIR

http://www.careerexpo.com/

Nationwide job and resume postings, library of career articles.

WORLD WIDE CAREER NETWORK

http://wwbc.com/english/careers/careers.html

Worldwide job postings and resume uploads.

MULTIMEDIA
CAREER PRODUCTS

Thanks to some forward-thinking publishers, you can turn your home into a job-seeking powerbase just by using your computer, VCR, television or audio cassette player. In this section, you will find listings for career-related:

◆ Computer Software and CD-ROMs

◆ Video and Audio Cassettes

◆ Job Search Tool Kits

◆ Cable Broadcasts

Here's what multimedia resources can do for you: Resume software can guide you in writing and formatting your resume using pre-designed templates. Some packages let you electronically manage your job search by tracking contacts and generating a daily to-do list. Other computerized career systems use interactive approaches to help you identify your strengths and ideal career choices. And, of course, there's no shortage of career advice on videos, audio tapes or cable programs.

If your budget is tight, borrow, don't buy. Look for multimedia resources at your public library or career centers sponsored by local job-coaching services. See Chapter One for listings.

Please note: The editors of the *Minnesota Job Seeker's Sourcebook* have not tested all products listed on the following pages. Descriptions are based on information provided to us by the publishers. Therefore we urge you to be a smart consumer. Ask about features, system requirements, shipping costs and return policies before purchasing.

SOFTWARE & CD-ROM

ACHIEVING YOUR CAREER™

Up Software, Inc.
722 Lombard St., Suite 204, San Francisco, CA 94133
(800) 959-8208

For Macintosh or IBM/compatible PC.

Resume templates, database of 800 national companies, calendars, contact and job lead tracking system, job-search tips. Call for additional system requirements. $69.95.

Also available from the Publisher:

Jumpstart Your Job Skills™: How to sell your skills in the job market. $69.95.

Building Your Job Search Foundation™: Strategies to strengthen the job search. $44.95.

CAREER DESIGN

Career Design
P.O. Box 2086, Sedona, AZ 86339
(800) 346-8007

Requires IBM or compatible PC.

Self-assessment exercises to focus on personal interests, skills and career goals. Modules to generate resumes and letters, job-search tips. $99.95.

CAREERPATH™

OnTrack Media
150B Shoreline Hwy., Suite 22, Mill Valley, CA 94941
(415) 331-1692   (800) 505-5627

Requires IBM or compatible PC, 386 or higher with Windows 3.1.

Helps user evaluate career choices by developing a personal career assessment profile. Matches interests, values, abilities and experience to ideally suited careers. Call for system requirements. $49.95.

CREATE YOUR DREAM JOB™

Wilson Learning Corp.
7500 Flying Cloud Dr., Eden Prairie, MN 55344
(800) 247-7332

For Macintosh, System 7.0 or higher; Requires CD-ROM drive.
For IBM or compatible with Windows 3.1; Requires CD-ROM drive.

CD ROM. Interactive program with full-motion video helps users examine talents, passions and purpose to envision their dream job. Call for additional system requirements. $49.95.

Also available from the Publisher:

Repacking Your Bags™: CD-ROM. How to take a fresh approach to your work and personal life. $49.95.

JOB FINDER'S TOOLKIT

Planning Communications
7215 Oak Ave., River Forest, IL 60305-1935
(800) 829-5220

Requires IBM or compatible PC with Windows 3.1 or higher.

Nationwide listings for job hotlines, trade periodicals, salary surveys, resume databases and more. Floppy disk, $79.95; CD ROM, $69.95.

JOB HUNT

Scope International
P.O. Box 25252, Charlotte, NC 28229
(800) 843-5627

Requires IBM or compatible PC with Windows 3.1 or higher.

Searchable database of over 10,000 companies with ability to create mailing lists. Built-in word processor. $49.95.

Also available from the Publisher:

Hit List. CD-ROM. Searchable profiles of 100,000 companies with ability to create mailing lists, resumes. $69.95.

To order multimedia products, contact the publishers directly or Resource Publishing Group at (612) 545-5980.

PFS: RESUME & JOB SEARCH PRO

Softkey International, Inc.
One Athenaeum St., Cambridge, MA 02142
(800) 227-5609

Requires IBM or compatible PC. DOS and Windows versions available.

Capability to customize templates to develop resumes and cover letters, print labels and envelopes. Includes contact manager, database of 6,000 U.S. companies, job-search tips. Call for additional system requirements. $49.95. Also available on CD-ROM.

QUICK & EASY FEDERAL JOBS KIT

DataTech Software
6360 Flank Dr., Harrisburg, PA 17112
(800) 377-3213

Requires IBM or compatible PC.

Helps prepare all forms required for applying for employment with the federal government: SF-171, OF-612, OF-306. Also includes required resume format for federal applications. Call for additional system requirements. $49.95.

Also available from the Publisher:

PowerWords. How to make more powerful presentations on federal job applications. $19.95.

READY TO GO RESUMES

Ten Speed Press
Box 7123, Berkeley, CA 94707
(800) 841-2665

For Macintosh or IBM/compatible PC. DOS and Windows versions.

Pre-designed resume templates have built-in resume-writing generator allowing user to quickly prepare a resume with step-by-step guidance. Requires Word Perfect or MS Word. Call for additional system requirements. $29.95.

RESUMEMAKER WITH CAREER PLANNING

Individual Software, Inc.
5870 Stoneridge Dr., #1, Pleasanton, CA 94588
(800) 331-3313

Available for Macintosh or IBM/compatible PC.

Provides templates to produce a variety of resume types and formats and customize letters. Also includes interview tips, appointment book and system to track activities and follow up. $19.95.

Also available from the Publisher:

ResumeMaker CD Deluxe. CD-ROM. Requires IBM or compatible PC with Windows; CD-ROM drive. Interactive career planning module, online video interviewing, resume templates, built-in word processor. $39.95.

SHARKWARE™

CogniTech Corporation
P.O. Box 500129, Atlanta, GA 31150
(800) 947-5075

Requires IBM or compatible PC, 386 or higher, with Windows 3.1.

Software to manage contacts and activities. Provides ability to store unlimited addresses and contacts with space for comments. Also includes to-do list, appointment calendar, telephone call manager. Call for additional system requirements. $199.95.

SUREFIRE RESUME FOR WINDOWS™

Cosmi
2600 Homestead Place, Rancho Dominguez, CA 90220
(310) 833-2000

Requires IBM/compatible, 386 or faster, with Windows 3.1 or higher.

Provides templates to create customized resumes, cover letters and thank you letters. Also includes built-in contact management system, job-search tips and sample resumes. $14.95.

To order multimedia products, contact the publishers directly or
Resource Publishing Group at (612) 545-5980.

THE PERFECT RESUME

Davidson & Associates, Inc.
P.O. Box 2961
Torrance, CA 90509
(800) 545-7677

For Macintosh with CD-ROM drive.

For IBM/compatible, 486 or faster, with Windows; CD-ROM drive.

CD-ROM. Online video job-search advice, resume templates, fill-in-the-blank cover-letters, database to track job-search contacts. Call for additional system requirements. $44.95.

THE ULTIMATE JOB SOURCE™

InfoBusiness, Inc.
887 South Orem Blvd., Orem, UT 84058-5009
(800) 657-5300

Requires IBM/compatible with Windows 3.1 or higher; CD-ROM drive.

CD-ROM. Interactive approach to help users identify skills and match them to database of 12,000 occupations. Also includes occupational profiles and outlooks, resume guide with word-processing capability, video job-search tips, contact manager, job search resources. $49.95.

WINWAY RESUME

WinWay Corporation
5431 Auburn Blvd., Suite 398, Sacramento, CA 95841-2801
(916) 965-7878
(800) 494-6929

Online product catalog: http://www.winway.com

Requires IBM or compatible PC with Windows 3.1 or higher.

Creates resumes and cover letters with choices of different styles and fonts. Also includes contact manager, interview simulation and salary negotiation advice. Call for additional system requirements. Available on floppy disk or CD-ROM. $39.95.

AUDIO & VIDEO

A PRACTICAL GUIDE TO FINDING A JOB IN TODAY'S FRENZIED MARKET

Maximum Potential
1440 South Priest, Suite 104, Tempe, AZ 85281
(800) 809-0165

Two audio cassettes. Running time: 90 minutes.

Offers a variety of work-search suggestions including job-finding strategies, resume-writing tips, guidelines for selecting references, advice on how to work effectively with recruiters and best ways to respond to ads. $8.50.

BASIC GUIDE TO RESUME WRITING AND JOB INTERVIEWS

Vocational Biographies
P.O. Box 31
Sauk Centre, MN 56378-0031
(800) 255-0752

Video cassette. Running time: 45 minutes.

Video guide to finding employment. Offers resume tips and interviewing examples written and produced by employment professionals. $89.00.

DOING WHAT YOU LOVE, LOVING WHAT YOU DO

Sound Editions from Random House
400 Hahn Road, Westminister, MD 21157
(800) 733-3000

Audio cassette. Running time: 90 minutes.

Variety of ideas on how to get more out of work by learning how to realistically set objectives, improve flexibility and working for your own approval. $11.00.

To order multimedia products, contact the publishers directly or Resource Publishing Group at (612) 545-5980.

50 WAYS TO GET HIRED

CareerTrack Publications
3085 Center Green Dr., Boulder, CO 80308
(800) 334-1018

Four audio cassettes. Running time: Three hours.

Learn how to showcase qualifications and convince employers you're the best fit for their needs, how to overcome objections. $49.95.

Also available from the Publisher:

Power Networking. How to expand professional and personal contacts. Four audio cassettes. Running time 3 hours, 38 minutes. $59.95.

Life by Design. How to take charge of your life and well-being. Four audio cassettes. Running time: Four hours, 6 minutes. $59.95.

JOB SHOCK:

How to be a Winner in the New Workplace

Audio Renaissance Tapes
5858 Wilshire Blvd., Suite 205, Los Angeles, CA 90036
(800) 288-2131

Audio cassette. Running time: Three hours.

How to survive and prosper from the job revolution and track down new responsibilities and opportunities. $16.95.

JOBSMARTS FOR TWENTYSOMETHINGS:

A Street-smart Script for Career Success

Random House Audio Books
New York, NY 10022
(800) 733-3000

Audio cassette. Running time: 60 minutes.

Advice by successful individuals in their 20s in a variety of fields on surviving office politics, hot careers, interviewing skills, how to deal with little or no experience and why to avoid newspaper ads. $11.00.

THE CAREER COACH

Dove Audio
301 North Canon Dr.
Beverly Hills, CA 90210
(800) 328-3683

Two audio cassettes. Running time: Three hours.

Tips on how to get and keep the job you want, excel in interviews and ask for a raise, balance home and work, prepare for a second career, tackle discrimination in the workplace. $17.95.

THE INSIDER'S GUIDE TO COMPETITIVE INTERVIEWING

WinWay Corporation
5431 Auburn Blvd., Suite 398, Sacramento, CA 95841-2801
(916) 965-7878   (800) 494-6929

Online product catalog: http://www.winway.com

Video cassette. Running time: 60 minutes.

Videotape of live lecture with tips on how to interview effectively with examples and scenarios. $39.95.

WHAT COLOR IS YOUR PARACHUTE?

Ten Speed Press
Box 7123, Berkeley, CA 94707
(800) 841-2665

Eight audio cassettes. Running time: Ten hours, 53 minutes.

Career guru Richard Nelson Bolles guides job seekers and career changers through a career exploration system based on his ever-popular guidebook. $50.00.

Also available from the Publisher:

Sweaty Palms: The Neglected Art of Being Interviewed. Presents real problems faced in job interviews and how to prepare for them using successful techniques. Audio cassette. Running time: 90 minutes. $12.95.

JOB SEARCH TOOL KITS

JOB SEEKER'S QUICKSTART TOOL KIT

Resource Publishing Group Inc.
P.O. Box 573, Hopkins, MN 55343
(612) 545-5980

Internet address: http://www.careerstore.com

Collection of job-seeking resources specifically designed for Minnesotans in job transition. Call for information and pricing. Tool Kit includes:

Job Seeker's Action Planner—Combination day-planner and goal-setting tool to help you focus your job search and stay on track. 40-page tablet.

Minnesota Job Seeker's Sourcebook—*This guidebook.*

Job Search Advisor—Quick-reading newsletters with best job-search tips.

Quick & Painless Cutbacks—Practical booklet with money-saving tips for surviving times of transition.

CABLE BROADCAST

CAREER CONVERSATIONS WITH SANDY KUNTZ©

Metro Cable Network Channel 6
Tuesdays, 7:30-8 p.m.

Direct inquiries about program content to:

ADVICE... 7964 Brooklyn Blvd., Suite 112, Brooklyn Park, MN 55445
(612) 560-2223

Locally produced talk show for Twin Cities viewing area. Featured guests share information about the changing world of work, hot careers, work-search skills, career resources and self-employment options. Special focus on Twin Cities job market. Videotapes of past broadcasts available. Also shown on Mondays at 8:30 p.m., Northwest Community Television, Channel 35.

LIBRARY & ONLINE

RESEARCH RESOURCES

In a tight job market, one way to stand above your competition is to gather facts like a pro. A little roll-up-your-sleeves research will provide you with current information about prospective employers, industry outlooks, authoritative do's and don'ts of the job search, salary surveys and up-and-coming careers.

It's no surprise that the library is the best place to start. Public, business, college and career libraries are gold mines of resources for job seekers. How-to books, business directories, software, audio tapes, videos, career guides, magazine articles, computer databases and Internet access are a few of the resources that may be available.

Serious researchers should look beyond the corner library. Locate the library in your area with the largest reference collection. The **James J. Hill Reference Library** in downtown St. Paul, (612) 227-9531, offers an impressive non-circulating collection of business resources and many electronic databases. Most college libraries are also open to the public although you may not be able to check out materials unless you have a student I.D. or alumni card. Don't overlook career libraries at colleges, universities, employment centers and outplacement firms. Many subscribe to hard-to-find career publications.

So, you say, you're not a world-class researcher. You can always hire the job done. James J. Hill (above) and **INFORM**, a research service sponsored by the **Minneapolis Public Library**, (612) 372-6636, conduct customized searches on all topics. Call for details.

LIBRARY RESEARCH RESOURCES

MINNESOTA CAREER INFORMATION SYSTEM (MCIS)
Minnesota Department of Children, Families and Learning
(612) 296-3653   (800) 599-6247

MCIS offers software and books about occupations, programs of study, financial aid and job-search strategies. Resources can be used, free, at technical and community colleges, employment centers, Minnesota Workforce Centers, some public libraries and other statewide locations.

MINNESOTA DIRECTORIES OF EMPLOYERS

The Brown Book
Twin Cities architectural, interior design, real estate and construction companies.

Corporate Report Fact Book
Minnesota public/private companies with 50+ employees. Includes brief background.

Dun's Regional Business Directory, Minneapolis/St. Paul
Businesses listed alphabetically, geographically, by SIC code. Brief background.

Medical Alley Directory
Minnesota healthcare manufacturing and service companies and major products.

Minneapolis Metro Business Directory
Twin City companies, key individuals, number of employees, SIC codes.

Minnesota Business Almanac
Minnesota public/private firms with brief background. Who's Who in Minnesota.

Minnesota Directory of Manufacturers
Listings include SIC codes and other background information.

Minnesota Manufacturers Register
Listings include SIC codes, scope of distribution, types of computers used.

Twin Cities Gold Book
Advertising, publishing, communications, creative services firms and area of focus.

Underwriters' Handbook of Minnesota
Insurance agencies, groups, field reps, general agents and adjusters.

CHAPTER THREE

FOR EMPLOYMENT
LEADS

- ◆ Job Hotlines
- ◆ Search & Temp Firms
- ◆ Resume Databases
- ◆ Recruitment Publications

If it's time to get serious about finding a job, listen up. There are more ways to track down positions available than waiting for the right job to surface in the Sunday want ads.

In this chapter, you will find resources that lead to actual job vacancies or attract potential employers. These resources include employer-sponsored job hotlines, search firms, employment agencies, temp and contract services, resume databases and recruitment publications.

Many professional associations also provide job leads to members. See page 228 for a sampling of Minnesota associations and networking groups. Internet employment resources provide access to hundreds of online databases with thousands of job opportunities. Check listings beginning on page 98.

Remember: many jobs are never advertised, and most people—about 85%—find work through networking. But don't let these statistics deter you from using job-lead services. A good strategy requires that you use every tool available to find the right job match.

JOB HOTLINES

♦♦♦♦♦

A telephone, a legal pad and a sharp pencil may be all you need to instantly access current information about job vacancies. Job hotlines sponsored by local corporations, government agencies and other organizations, provide free recorded messages that highlight the duties, salary ranges, application procedures and other requirements for available positions.

The amount and type of information varies among organizations. Most listings are updated weekly.

Here are some other quick tips when accessing a job hotline:

◆ Have pen and paper in hand: Information comes quickly.

◆ Some job hotlines require the use of a touch-tone phone but options are generally provided for rotary phone callers.

◆ Unless you don't mind hitting your redial button, call popular numbers like the Career America Connection, a federal job hotline, during evenings or weekends.

◆ Hotline numbers change frequently. If you reach a number that is no longer in service, call the organization's human resources department and ask for updated information.

ACCOUNTING ACTION LINE

(612) 773-0648

Recorded listing of accounting positions at Accounting Placement Registry, a Minneapolis search firm. Listing includes job description and salary ranges.

ADC TELECOMMUNICATIONS

(612) 946-3747

Recorded information lists job titles, requirements and application instructions. Updated weekly.

ADVANCE CIRCUITS INC.

(612) 930-8800

Recorded listing includes job titles, position requirements and instructions for how to apply.

AETNA HEALTH PLANS

(612) 399-2574

Recorded message describes current job openings and instructions about the application process.

AMERICAN ASSOCIATION OF LAW LIBRARIES

(312) 939-7877

Recorded message includes job descriptions, locations, requirements, salary ranges and application instructions for jobs throughout U.S. Job hotline is updated weekly.

AMERICAN EXPRESS FINANCIAL ADVISORS

(612) 671-5059

Recorded message lists current job descriptions, salary ranges, requirements and application process.

ANOKA COUNTY
(612) 422-7498

Recorded message lists job descriptions, requirements, salary ranges.

AT & T WIRELESS
(800) 438-3151

Recorded information lists job descriptions, requirements, locations and application instructions.

BANKERS SYSTEMS—ST. CLOUD
(320) 251-6114

Recorded listing of job descriptions, requirements and instructions for how to apply.

BARR ENGINEERING
(612) 832-2600

Ask for job hotline. Recorded listing of job titles and instructions for how to apply.

BEST BUY
(612) 947-2555

Recorded message describes current job openings and application instructions. Updated weekly.

BETHEL COLLEGE AND SEMINARY
(612) 635-8633

Recorded listing of current jobs, requirements and salary ranges.

BLUE CROSS / BLUE SHIELD OF MINNESOTA
(612) 456-8020

Recorded message includes job descriptions, requirements and application procedure. Updated weekly.

BRUEGGER'S BAGEL BAKERY
(612) 282-0228

Recorded information includes current job openings and locations.

CAREER AMERICA CONNECTION
U.S. Office of Personnel Management
(912) 757-3000

Student Hotline and General Hotline. Recordings list jobs nationwide with federal government, providing locations, salary ranges and instructions for how to apply.

CARGILL
(612) 742-2888

Recording lists job descriptions, requirements and instructions for application procedure.

CARLSON MARKETING GROUP
(612) 449-1111

Recorded listing of job descriptions, requirements and instructions for the application procedure.

CARVER COUNTY
(612) 361-1522

Recorded message lists job descriptions, requirements, locations, salary ranges and application instructions.

CENTRAL INTELLIGENCE AGENCY
(800) 562-7242

Recorded message includes current job descriptions, requirements and application instructions.

CHARTER MEDICAL CORP.
(800) 334-5392

Ask for career line. Recorded message lists job openings, requirements, locations and application instructions. Updated weekly.

CHOICE HOTEL INTERNATIONAL / MANOR CARE INC.
(800) 348-2041

Recorded message lists current job openings, locations and instructions for how to apply.

CITY OF BURNSVILLE
(612) 895-4475

Recorded job descriptions, salary ranges and application procedures.

CITY OF MINNEAPOLIS
(612) 673-2489

Recorded listing of job openings, requirements and description of application procedures. Updated bi-weekly.

CITY OF ST. PAUL
(612) 266-6502

Recorded job descriptions, salary ranges, application procedures.

COLLEGE OF ST. CATHERINE
(612) 690-6425

Recorded listings of job descriptions, requirements and application instructions. Updated weekly.

CYPRESS SEMICONDUCTOR
(612) 851-2975

Recorded listings of job descriptions, requirements, hours and instructions for how to apply.

DAKOTA COUNTY

(612) 438-4473

Recorded message describes weekly postings of Dakota County jobs. Recording provides job titles and salary ranges. Updated weekly.

DAMARK INTERNATIONAL

(612) 531-4562

Recorded information lists current job openings and instructions about how to apply.

DATACARD

(612) 931-1990

Recorded message provides job descriptions, requirements and application process. Updated weekly.

DAYTON'S EMPLOYMENT

(612) 375-4288

(800) 590-4473

Recorded listing of current job openings and application process. Updated weekly.

DELUXE CORPORATION

(612) 481-4100

Recorded listing of current job openings, qualifications required and application process.

ECOLAB INC.

(612) 293-4473

Recorded listing of current job openings and application process. Updated weekly.

EDEN PRAIRIE SCHOOL DISTRICT

(612) 975-7109/Non-Teaching   (612) 975-7108/Teaching

Ask for hotline. Recorded information about teaching and other positions available within Eden Prairie school district.

EDITORIAL FREELANCE ASSOCIATION

(212) 929-5411

The public can access this job hotline to hear recorded general information about freelance opportunities nationwide, but only members can receive detailed descriptions of positions. Updated weekly. Membership, $20 per year.

FAIRVIEW RIDGES HOSPITAL

(612) 892-2050

Ask for job hotline. Recorded information about job descriptions, hours and application instructions. Updated weekly.

FAIRVIEW RIVERSIDE MEDICAL CENTER

(612) 672-5627

Recorded information about current job vacancies, requirements and instructions on how to apply. Updated weekly.

FEDERAL CARTRIDGE

(612) 323-3863

Recorded message includes current job openings, qualifications required and application procedures.

FEDERAL RESERVE BANK OF MINNEAPOLIS

(612) 340-2120

Recorded information lists positions available, job descriptions, requirements and application procedure.

FINGERHUT

(320) 654-5627

Recorded information lists current job descriptions, requirements, locations and application procedures.

FLEMING, MINNEAPOLIS DIVISION

(612) 782-4492

Recorded message lists current job descriptions, requirements, salary ranges and application procedures.

FLUOROWARE

(612) 368-8088

Recorded message lists job openings, salary ranges and how to apply.

GENERAL MILLS

(612) 540-2334

Recorded message provides general instructions on how to apply for a position.

GILLETTE COMPANY

(612) 292-2924

Recorded information includes current job vacancies and instructions for application process.

GRACO

(612) 623-6389

Recorded message with job vacancies, application process. Updated weekly.

GREEN TREE FINANCIAL CORPORATION

(612) 293-5825

Recorded message lists job descriptions, requirements and application process. Updated weekly.

HAMLINE UNIVERSITY
(612) 659-3046

Recorded information includes job descriptions, requirements, salary ranges and application process. Updated weekly.

HEALTH RISK MANAGEMENT
(612) 829-3500 ext. 3695

Leave name and address on machine to receive application form.

HEALTH SYSTEMS INTEGRATION
(612) 858-7958

Recorded information lists current job descriptions, requirements and application instructions.

HEALTHEAST
(612) 232-1450

Recorded information includes job descriptions, requirements, locations and application instructions. Updated weekly.

HENNEPIN COUNTY
(612) 348-4698

Recorded message describes job openings, salary ranges, requirements and application procedures. Updated weekly.

HOFFMAN ENGINEERING
(612) 422-2559

Recorded message describes job vacancies and application procedures.

HONEYWELL
(612) 951-2914

Recorded message describes current job openings, descriptions, location, requirements and application instructions.

HUBBARD BROADCASTING

(612) 645-6060 Category 1919

Recorded job listings, requirements and directions on how to apply.

HYATT REGENCY, MINNEAPOLIS

(612) 370-1202

Recorded message lists current job descriptions, requirements, hours and directions on how to apply. Updated weekly.

IBM—ROCHESTER

(800) 964-4473

Recorded information lists current job vacancies.

IDX

(802) 865-0413

Recorded message lists current job descriptions, location, requirements and application process.

INDEPENDENT SCHOOL DISTRICT 281

(612) 533-2781

Ask for job hotline. Recorded information lists current job vacancies, descriptions and application process.

INTERNATIONAL DAIRY QUEEN INC.

(612) 896-8675

Recorded information lists current jobs, requirements, how to apply.

KARE 11 TELEVISION

(612) 546-1111 ext. 465

Recorded message lists current job descriptions, requirements and application process.

LAKEVIEW MEMORIAL HOSPITAL

(612) 430-4765

Recorded listing of current job descriptions, requirements and instructions for how to apply.

LAND O' LAKES / CENEX

(612) 481-2250

Recorded information includes job descriptions for current openings, locations, requirements, salary ranges and application procedures. Job hotline is updated weekly.

LIBERTY DIVERSIFIED INDUSTRIES

(612) 536-6656

Recorded message includes listings for current job openings and application instructions.

LITTLE SIX CASINO (MYSTIC LAKE)

(612) 496-6960

Recorded listing describes current job opportunities and information about the application procedures.

MACALESTER COLLEGE

(612) 696-6400

Recorded information includes current job descriptions, requirements, locations and application procedures.

MARQUETTE BANCSHARES, INC.

(612) 661-3838

Recorded message lists current job opportunities including position descriptions, salary ranges, qualifications required and instructions about how to apply.

MARRIOTT

(612) 349-4077—City Center

(612) 854-3809—Bloomington

Recorded message lists current job descriptions, salary ranges, requirements and application process.

MAYO FOUNDATION—ROCHESTER

(507) 284-2500

Call after 4 p.m. Listings include current job descriptions, locations, requirements and application process.

MCGLYNN BAKERY

(612) 574-2222

Ask for job hotline. Recorded information describes job descriptions and provides information about application procedures.

MCI

(800) 274-5758—Business Markets

(800) 888-2413—International

(800) 456-5243—Network Services

Recorded listings include current job opportunities, requirements, locations and application procedures.

MEDICAL LIBRARY ASSOCIATION

(312) 553-4636

Recorded message lists current job descriptions, locations, salary ranges and application instructions.

MEDTRONIC INC.

(612) 586-7724

Recording describes job openings and application instructions.

MESABA AVIATION

(612) 726-5155

Recorded job openings, requirements, how to apply. Updated weekly.

METROPOLITAN COUNCIL TRANSIT OPERATIONS

(612) 349-7557

Recorded message describes general hiring needs, how to apply.

MIDWEST COCA-COLA BOTTLING COMPANY

(612) 454-5460

Ask for job hotline. Recorded message lists current job descriptions, requirements, salary ranges and application instructions.

MINNEAPOLIS CHILDREN'S MEDICAL CENTER

(612) 813-6400

Recorded message describes job descriptions, requirements and application procedures. Updated weekly.

MINNEAPOLIS POST OFFICE

(612) 349-9100 message 811

Recorded information includes listing of exams offered statewide by the Postal Service for new entrants.

MINNEGASCO

(612) 321-4666

Recorded listing of job vacancies specifying job titles, descriptions and qualifications. Updated weekly.

MINNESOTA DEPARTMENT OF EMPLOYEE RELATIONS

(612) 296-2616   (612) 296-6700

Recording describes current job vacancies, salary ranges, requirements and application instructions for state government jobs.

MINNESOTA MUTUAL LIFE INSURANCE
(612) 298-7934

Recorded message for office/technical positions. Application information is provided for professional and managerial positions.

MINNESOTA POWER—DULUTH
(218) 722-2641 ext. 3068

Recorded information lists current job descriptions, application instructions.

MINNESOTA TECHNICAL SERVICES ASSOCIATION
(612) 362-3660

Recorded information about job descriptions, locations, salary ranges, application instructions.

MINNESOTA TELECOMMUNICATIONS ASSOCIATION
(612) 671-7333

Recorded information includes job descriptions and instructions for how to apply.

MINNESOTA WOMEN IN THE TRADES
(612) 228-1271

Recorded job descriptions, locations, salary ranges and how to apply.

MOUNDSVIEW SCHOOLS
(612) 636-3656 ext. 1100

Recorded message includes description of job openings and application procedures. Updated weekly.

MSI INSURANCE
(612) 639-5500

Recorded message includes job descriptions, requirements and application process. Updated weekly.

MULTIFOODS

(612) 340-3923

Recorded message includes current job vacancies and application procedures.

MUSICLAND GROUP

(612) 932-7700

Ask for job hotline. Recorded message describes application instructions.

92 KQRS

(612) 881-4636 ext. 92

Recording describes job openings with different companies throughout the Twin Cities. Message includes job titles, locations, application instructions.

NATIONAL COMPUTER SYSTEMS

(612) 829-3005

Recorded information describes job descriptions, requirements and application process. Updated weekly.

NATIONAL HEALTH CAREERS

(800) 999-4248

Leave a message on machine to receive information.

NETWORK SYSTEMS CORP.

(612) 424-4888

Ask for job hotline. Leave name and number on machine to receive information about current job openings.

NORDICTRACK INC.

(612) 368-2562

Recorded information lists current job descriptions, requirements and application instructions.

NORTHERN STATES POWER

(612) 330-7800   (800) 328-8226 ext. 7800

Recorded message provides general information on how to apply for employment. Updated bi-weekly.

NORTHERN TELECOM

(800) 667-8437   Press 4 during business hours

Recorded information lists job titles and application procedures.

NORTHWEST AIRLINES

(612) 726-3600

Recorded message describes hiring needs and instructions for general application procedures.

NORTHWEST RACQUET, SWIM & HEALTH CLUBS

(612) 673-1229

Recorded message includes job descriptions, requirements, locations and application process. Updated weekly.

NORWEST BANK

(612) 667-5627

Recorded job vacancies at numerous bank locations. Updated weekly.

PACE INC.

(612) 525-3480

Recorded message lists current job descriptions, requirements and directions on how to apply.

PETSMART

(800) 899-7387

Recorded information lists current job descriptions, requirements, location and application instructions.

PILLSBURY

(612) 330-4302

Recorded message describes general application procedures. Most job vacancies are filled by internal transfers and promotions.

PIPER JAFFRAY COMPANY

(612) 342-1099

Recorded message of job descriptions, salary ranges, requirements and application procedures. General listings include entry level and experienced professional positions. Updated weekly.

PRUDENTIAL INSURANCE COMPANY

Minneapolis Office

(612) 553-5991

Recorded message provides job titles, salary ranges and brief descriptions. Updated weekly.

RADISSON SOUTH

(612) 893-8416

Recorded listings describe current job vacancies and application process. Updated weekly.

RAMSEY COUNTY

(612) 266-2666

Recorded information includes job descriptions, requirements and instructions for applying.

RELIASTAR FINANCIAL CORPORATION

(612) 342-3594

Recorded message includes job description and instructions for applying for employment.

ROLLERBLADE

(612) 930-7003

Recorded information lists current job titles, requirements and application instructions. Updated weekly.

ROOTS & FRUITS PRODUCE

(612) 722-9271   ext. 777

Recorded message includes current jobs, requirements, salary ranges.

ST. MARY'S MEDICAL CENTER—DULUTH

(218) 725-7266

Recorded message lists current job descriptions, requirements, hours and application instructions. Updated weekly.

ST. PAUL PIONEER PRESS

(612) 228-5008

Recorded message lists current positions available, job descriptions, qualifications, salary ranges and hours required.

ST. PAUL POST OFFICE

(612) 349-9100 Message #811

Recorded message includes schedule of exams offered statewide by the Postal Service for new entrants.

ST. PAUL RAMSEY MEDICAL CENTER

(612) 221-4302

Recorded message includes requirements, salary ranges, how to apply.

SCIENCE MUSEUM OF MINNESOTA

(612) 221-9488

Recorded message includes current job descriptions, qualifications and requirements, salary ranges and instructions on how to apply.

SCIMED LIFE SYSTEMS

(612) 494-2600 ext. 5627

Recorded message includes current job vacancies and instructions on how to apply.

SCOTT COUNTY

(612) 496-8598

Recorded message includes current job descriptions, requirements, hours, salary ranges and application instructions. Updated weekly.

SPECIAL LIBRARIES ASSOCIATION

(202) 234-4700 ext. 1

Recorded message lists nationwide job descriptions, locations, salary ranges, requirements, how to apply. Updated bi-weekly.

STAR TRIBUNE

(612) 673-4075

Recorded listings of job descriptions, qualifications, salary ranges and hours. Updated bi-weekly.

STARKEY LABORATORIES

(800) 328-8604

Recorded job openings, requirements, how to apply. Updated weekly.

SUNDT CORPORATION

(800) 873-6078

Recorded listing of current job titles, locations and application instructions.

SUPERAMERICA GROUP INC.

(612) 887-6160

Message lists instructions on how to apply.

SUPERVALU

(612) 932-4777

Recorded message lists current job descriptions, requirements, salary ranges and application procedures.

SYSCO MINNESOTA

(612) 783-1007

Taped listing of current jobs, requirements, how to apply. Updated weekly.

TCF BANK

(612) 661-8989

Recorded message includes job descriptions, requirements, locations, hours and application instructions. Updated weekly.

TARGET HEADQUARTERS

(612) 304-4960

Recorded message about current job openings and application process.

TIRES PLUS

(612) 895-4908

Leave name, number and position desired on machine to receive information.

TORO COMPANY

(612) 887-7300

Recorded information lists job descriptions, requirements and application instructions. Updated weekly.

TWIN CITIES CAREER AMERICA CONNECTION

(612) 725-3430

Taped message describes job vacancies with federal government, locations and how to apply.

TWIN CITIES PERSONNEL ASSOCIATION

(612) 832-3898

Recording describes job vacancies, locations, requirements and application process. Updated weekly.

TWIN CITIES PUBLIC TELEVISION

(612) 229-1127

Recorded message lists job descriptions, requirements, salary ranges and application instructions. Updated bi-weekly.

UNITED FOR EXCELLENCE INC.

(612) 439-1561

Ask for jobline. Recording lists current jobs, how to apply.

UNITED HOSPITAL

(612) 220-5627

Information includes job descriptions, requirements. Updated weekly.

UNITED STATES DEPARTMENT OF INTERIOR

(800) 336-4562

Listings include current job descriptions, requirements, location and application instructions.

UNITED STATES DEPARTMENT OF LABOR

(800) 336-2753

Recorded message includes job descriptions, locations and directions on how to apply. Updated weekly.

UNITED STATES PEACE CORPS

(800) 424-8580

Recorded message gives instructions for contacting local Peace Corp offices for information about employment opportunities.

UNIVERSITY OF MINNESOTA

(612) 645-6060 Category 2500

Recorded message describes wide variety of job opportunities with qualifications and salary ranges.

UNIVERSITY OF MINNESOTA—DULUTH

(218) 726-6506

Recording lists current job descriptions and application instructions.

UNIVERSITY OF ST. THOMAS

(612) 962-6520

Recorded message includes job descriptions, requirements and instructions on how to apply. Updated weekly.

VALUE VISION

(612) 947-5222

Recorded information lists general application procedures.

VAUGHN COMMUNICATIONS

(612) 832-3260

Recorded message includes current job vacancies, descriptions, locations, requirements and application procedures.

WCCO TELEVISION

(612) 339-4444

Ask for jobline. Recorded information describes current job descriptions, requirements and application procedures.

WALKER ART CENTER

(612) 375-7588

Recorded message lists current job vacancies, how to apply.

WALKER METHODIST INC.

(612) 827-5931

Ask for job hotline. Information highlights current job titles, hours and how to apply.

WASHINGTON COUNTY

(612) 430-6084

Recorded message provides job description and salary ranges.

WAUSAU INSURANCE COMPANY

(612) 820-3413

Recorded message describes current job opportunities and instructions on how to apply.

WILDER FOUNDATION

(612) 642-2087

Recorded message includes job descriptions, locations, requirements and application process. Updated weekly.

WRIGHT COUNTY

(612) 682-7454

Recorded job descriptions, requirements, salary ranges and how to apply.

SEARCH & TEMP
FIRMS

Search and temporary help firms can be useful gateways to your next permanent job. In this section, you will find listings for:

◆ Search Firms
◆ Employment Agencies
◆ Contract Employers
◆ Temporary Placement Services

SEARCH FIRMS & EMPLOYMENT AGENCIES

Before you mail off your resume to every search firm and employment agency in the Yellow Pages, let's put to rest the confusion between these two types of organizations and what they can do for you.

Employment agencies are placement services that typically work with recent college graduates or hourly personnel to help them find suitable positions. Employment agencies in Minnesota must be licensed by the state and are permitted to charge fees to job seekers, to employers or to both. Applicants can request to see only those positions with employer-paid fees.

Search firms (also referred to as "headhunters") are recruitment services usually geared to seeking out candidates for highly compensated positions, $50,000 or more. Search firms must be registered with the state and cannot charge fees to job seekers.

There are two types of search firms: retainer and contingency. A retainer search firm is hired by a company to recruit candidates for high level positions. Retainer firms are paid whether or not they find a suitable match.

A contingency firm, on the other hand, is given a work order by an employer and asked to fill an opening. Several competing contingency firms may receive the same work order. These firms are paid only if the position is filled.

Both types of firms have focused assignments. They work for employers to scour the job market for specific candidates for specific job openings. They are not in business to market job seekers to potential employers. As such, some do not welcome cold calls from individuals.

How to work with Search Firms and Employment Agencies

◆ Most recruitment firms specialize in a particular field, industry or occupational level. Investigate which organizations specialize in your area, then contact each one.

◆ Is the organization an employment agency or search firm? If in doubt, call the **Minnesota Department of Labor and Industry**, Division of Labor Standards, (612) 296-2282. Remember: an employment agency can charge you a fee; search firms cannot.

◆ Clarify whether the firm works on a contingency or retainer basis. Contingency firms may be more receptive to cold calls from job seekers, and more willing to keep your name for future opportunities.

◆ To contact a firm in this book, follow the advice they have provided about how to apply. A good rule of thumb is to mail, E-mail or fax your resume and salary parameters, then follow up by phone.

◆ Clarify the firm's policy on confidentiality. Ask if your resume will be faxed throughout the industry or posted on an online database.

◆ Today, many search firms use computer technology to scan applicant resumes for keywords—skills, training, work experience, education, etc.—that match the employer's desired or required qualifications for a specific job.

Before sending your resume to a recruiter, learn how to prepare a "scannable" version of your resume. Several good books can explain the process including **Electronic Resume Revolution** by Joyce Lain Kennedy (John Wiley & Sons) and **Electronic Resumes for the New Job Market** by Peter Weddle (Impact Publications).

◆ Career changers, don't look to recruitment services. Recruiters are primarily interested in your *proven* track record and industry knowledge—not in your career potential.

◆ With limited space, we are unable to list every recruitment service in Minnesota. For more listings, check your local bookstore or library for these guides: **The Directory of Executive Recruiters** (Kennedy Publications), **The Job Seeker's Guide to Executive Recruiters** (Hunt-Scanlon Publishing), **The Best Directory of Recruiters, Agencies and Consultants** (Gove Publishing Company), **The Career Makers: America's Top 100 Executive Recruiters** (Harper & Row).

◆ If you want a quick response from a recruiter confirming that your resume was received or whether your qualifications match any current prospects, enclose a self-addressed, stamped postcard when mailing your resume.

◆ Keep in mind that surveys indicate that less than 10 percent of all job seekers land jobs through recruitment services. Be realistic about the role these organizations may play in your overall strategy.

TEMPORARY & CONTRACT FIRMS

Here's an astonishing fact: By the year 2000, one in three U.S. workers will make a living outside the traditional workplace. That estimate includes part-time employees, the self-employed and temporary workers. **Temporary employment** is a multi-billion dollar industry—and growing.

Employers are turning to temporary workers to fill some of their ranks. The practice of using temps may not be heartening to individuals seeking permanent work but there's good news too.

Gone are the days when a temp worker was the fill-in receptionist at the front desk. Today temp opportunities also exist for managers, professionals and executives. Assignments may range from one day to several years. According to the National Association of Temporary Staffing Services, the number of assignments for temporary professionals nearly tripled between 1991-95.

For those out of work—especially those who are ages 40 or 50 something—temporary jobs can provide many benefits. Interim income. A structured daily routine. The opportunity to stay professionally active. A fresh and expanding network of contacts. Flexible scheduling that allows for continuing job-seeking efforts. And the chance to "try out" different employers.

Likewise, employers use temporary assignments as a no-risk way to try out new workers. These trial relationships often have happy endings. Many temp employees are subsequently hired on a permanent basis.

In contrast to temporary employment, **contract employment** is another interim work option characterized by longer-term, project-based assignments. Contract employment is generally geared to highly trained personnel in engineering, computer engineering, technical writing and other areas.

In recent years, contract opportunities have broadened beyond the technical sphere. It is not uncommon today to encounter contract workers in accounting, finance, sales and management areas.

Tips on working with Temp and Contract Firms

◆ Be selective about which firms you approach. Clarify the type of work you want, your acceptable salary level or wage, the days or times you can work, how far you're willing to travel and the duration of an assignment you're willing to accept.

◆ Request a written agreement specifying the details of each assignment.

◆ If you're currently receiving reemployment compensation, a contract or temp position could affect your continuing eligibility for benefits. Call your local Job Service/Reemployment office and ask a representative to clarify the guidelines.

◆ **PLEASE NOTE:** The **Minnesota Association of Personnel Services** (MAPS) is a statewide organization that sets forth ethical standards for its member firms which include search, employment and temporary services. To obtain a list of MAPS members, or to inquire about the association's grievance or arbitration procedures, call (612) 835-4333.

ACCOUNTANTS EXCHANGE, INC.

2233 Hamline Ave. No., Suite 509
Roseville, MN 55113
(612) 636-5490   Fax—(612) 636-8799

Search firm. Specializes in recruitment for all positions in accounting and financial fields. Mail resume; follow up by phone. Fees paid by employer.

ACCOUNTANTS EXECUTIVE SEARCH

45 So. 7th St., Suite 3004
Minneapolis, MN 55402
(612) 341-9900   Fax—(612) 341-3284

Search firm. Placement of accountants, financial analysts and other high-level positions in the financial field. Call for information. Fees paid by employer.

ACCOUNTANTS ON CALL

45 So. 7th St., Suite 3004
Minneapolis, MN 55402
(612) 341-9900   Fax—(612) 341-3284

Search firm. Specializes in permanent and temporary placement of accountants at all levels. Call for information or to schedule an appointment. Fees paid by employer.

ACCOUNTANTS PLACEMENT REGISTRY

1703 Cope Avenue
Maplewood, MN 55109
(612) 773-9018
Fax—(612) 773-8071

Search firm. Specializes in permanent and contract positions in accounting and finance for controllers, CFO's, bookkeepers, accountants, accounting managers and financial analysts. Call for information. Fees paid by employer.

ADVANCE PERSONNEL RESOURCES

715 Florida Ave., Suite 301
Minneapolis, MN 55426
(612) 546-6779   Fax—(612) 546-2523

Search firm. Specializes in permanent placement of sales professionals and managers, marketing personnel, manufacturing managers, experienced administrators. Fees paid by employer.

ADVANCE / POSSIS TECHNICAL STAFFING

3131 Fernbrook Lane, Suite 100
Minneapolis, MN 55447
(612) 577-9000   Fax—(612) 577-9010

Offers contract, temp, temp-to-perm and permanent placement for engineering, drafting, design, computer engineering and technical writing personnel. Mail resume; follow up by phone. No applicant fees.

ADVANCED PERSONNEL PLACEMENT

2499 Rice St., Suite 206
St. Paul, MN 55113
(612) 481-9709   Fax—(612) 481-7821

Search firm. Permanent placement of experienced workers through mid-management in food industry. Positions in CAD, CAM, CNC, mortgage banking, office occupations, customer service. Call for appointment. Fees paid by employer.

AGRI SEARCH

7550 France Ave. So., Suite 180
Minneapolis, MN 55435
(612) 830-1569   Fax—(612) 893-9254
E-mail: manager@MRINET.com

Search firm. Specializes in permanent placement of sales, management and technical personnel in agriculture industry. Call for appointment. Fees paid by employer.

AGRO QUALITY SEARCH INC.

7260 University Ave. N.E., Suite 305
Minneapolis, MN 55432
(612) 572-3737   Fax—(612) 572-3738

Search firm. Permanent placement of personnel in management, sales, marketing, technical, production and service areas of the agriculture/food industries. Mail resume; follow up by phone. Fees paid by employer.

ALLIED PROFESSIONALS

3209 W. 76th Street, Suite 201
Edina, MN 55435
(612) 832-5101   Fax—(612) 832-0656

Temporary medical staffing for experienced nurses, dentists, nursing/medical assistants, lab and x-ray techs, home health aides, support staff. Call for appointment. No fees to applicant.

ALTERNATIVE STAFFING, INC.

8120 Penn Ave. So., Suite 570
Bloomington, MN 55431
(612) 888-6077   Fax—(612) 888-6153

Search firm. Specializes in permanent and temporary placement of office support, accounting, mortgage personnel. Call for appointment. Fees paid by employer.

ANDCOR HUMAN RESOURCES

600 U.S. Hwy. 169, Suite 1150
Minneapolis, MN 55426
(612) 546-0966   Fax—(612) 593-8968
Internet address: http://www.andcor.com
E-Mail: keller@andcor.com

Permanent and contract placements of technical and non-technical personnel in sales, marketing, human resources, finance. Mail resume; follow up by phone. No applicant fees.

BEMEL & HENSON

708 No. First Street, Suite 236
Minneapolis, MN 55401
(612) 673-0020   Fax—(612) 673-0588

Search firm. Serving professionals and mid- to upper management in marketing, sales, human resources, finance and general management in a variety of industries. Fax resume; follow up by phone. No fees to applicant.

BRIGHT SEARCH / PROFESSIONAL STAFFING

8120 Penn Ave. So.
Minneapolis, MN 55431
(612) 884-8111

Search firm. Recruits and markets professionals in sales, marketing, engineering, technical specialties, general management. Provides nationwide coverage with associate agencies. Mail resume and salary requirements. No applicant fees.

BUSINESS TALENT / INSURANCE TALENT

P.O. Box 40064
St. Paul, MN 55104
(612) 690-0695   Fax—(612) 699-1193

Retained search firm. Recruits for sales and underwriting professionals in property and casualty insurance. Specializes in sales, marketing, management and tech positions in diverse industries. Mail or fax resume. No applicant fees.

CAREER CENTERS, INC.

7300 France Ave. So., Suite 210
Edina, MN 55435
(612) 835-7771   Fax—(612) 835-3205

Search firm. Specializes in the recruitment of experienced sales personnel. Call for appointment. Fees paid by employer.

CAREER PROFESSIONALS, INC.

4930 W. 77th Street, Suite 260
Edina, MN 55435
(612) 835-9922   Fax—(612) 835-0851

Employment agency. Specializes in recruiting for entry level career positions and placements of recent college grads with 0—5 years post college work experience. Call for appointment. Generally fees are paid by the employer.

CDI CORPORATION

5775 Wayzata Blvd., Suite 875
St. Louis Park, MN 55416
(612) 541-9967   Fax—(612) 541-9605

Contract staffing service. Specializes in placements for information services and engineering. No fees to applicant.

CENTURY DESIGN INC.

530 15th Ave. So.
Hopkins, MN 55343
(612) 935-0033   Fax—(612) 935-4295

Contract, temporary and temp-to-perm positions for technical writers/ editors, illustrators, desktop publishers, instructional designers and developers, multimedia specialists. Mail resume; follow up by phone. No fees to applicant.

COMPU-SEARCH INC.

7550 France Avenue So., Suite 180
Minneapolis, MN 55435
(612) 830-1135   Fax—(612) 893-9254

Search firm. Specializes in placements of technical and mid-management personnel in data processing. Call to schedule an appointment. Fees are paid by the employer.

COMPUTER PERSONNEL R PARTNERS

5353 Wayzata Blvd., Suite 604
Minneapolis, MN 55416
(612) 542-8053   (800) 264-8053   Fax—(612) 542-9056
E-mail: Bostka@winternet.com

Search firm. Permanent placements for all levels of positions in the computer industry. Call for appointment. Fees paid by employer.

CONSOLIDATED SERVICES

10125 Crosstown Circle, Suite 230
Eden Prairie, MN 55344
(612) 941-0149   Fax—(612) 941-6983

Contract and temporary employment service. Specializes in engineering and medical industry. Positions for drafters, designers, software engineers, programmers, system analysts, tech writers, etc. Mail or fax resume. No fees to applicant.

DACON ENGINEERING AND SERVICE COMPANY, INC.

4915 W. 35th Street
Minneapolis, MN 55416
(612) 920-8040   Fax—(612) 920-7619

Contract employment service. Specializes in engineering and technical positions. Mail or fax resume; follow up by phone. No fees to applicant.

DASHE & THOMSON TECHNICAL WRITING CONSULTANTS

401 No. Third St., Suite 500
Minneapolis, MN 55401
(612) 338-4911
Fax—(612) 338-4920

Contract employment service. Specializes in positions for Fortune 500 companies including technical writers, editors, illustrators and desktop publishers. Mail resume; follow up by phone. No fees to applicant.

DEVELOPMENT RESOURCE GROUP

2722 Hwy. 694, Suite 105
New Brighton, MN 55112
(612) 636-9141   Fax—(612) 636-9312

Contract employment service. Specializes in electronics industry with focus on biomedical. Positions for hardware/software engineers, technicians and principal design engineers. Call for information.

DISTINCTION IN DESIGN

14264 23rd Ave. No.
Plymouth, MN 55447
(612) 550-1138   Fax—(612) 550-1349

Contract and permanent employment opportunities in high-tech engineering and manufacturing. Positions for engineers, design drafters, technicians and software engineers. Mail resume; follow up by phone. No fees to applicant.

DIVERSIFIED EMPLOYMENT INC.

4825 Olson Memorial Highway, Suite 101
Golden Valley, MN 55422
(612) 546-8255   Fax—(612) 546-4106

Search firm. Placement services for college and entry level, production, technical and support staff. Industry specialities include manufacturing, engineering, computer, construction and printing. Fax resume or call for appointment. No fees to applicant.

ELLS PERSONNEL

9900 Bren Road E., Suite 105
Minneapolis, MN 55343
(612) 932-9933   (800) 328-4827 ext. 1164   Fax—(612) 932-0099

Search firm. Permanent and contract positions in building products, engineering, medical, office support, printing. Mail resume; follow up by phone. No fees to applicant.

ENGINEERING AND COMPUTER PROFESSIONALS INC.

2305 Lilac Lane
St. Paul, MN 55110-7424
(612) 429-0101   Fax—(612) 429-4064

Search firm and contract employment. Serving personnel in manufacturing. Positions for engineers, computer scientists, designers, drafters, technicians, skilled trades. Fax/mail resume; follow up by phone. No applicant fees.

ENGINEERING RESOURCES OF MINNESOTA

1315 Rice Creek Road
Fridley, MN 55432
(612) 572-0415   Fax—(612) 572-2433

Contract and permanent employment. Specializes in engineering industry. Positions for drafters, programmers, engineers and technicians. Mail resume; follow up by phone. No applicant fees.

ESP SYSTEMS PROFESSIONALS, INC.

701 Fourth Ave. So., Suite 1800
Minneapolis, MN 55415
(612) 337-3000   Fax—(612) 337-9199
Internet address: http://www.esp.com
E-mail: careers@esp.com

Search firm, contract employment. Specializes in data processing industry. Positions for programmers, systems and programmer analysts, project leaders, systems programmers. Mail resume. No applicant fees.

EXECU-TECH SEARCH, INC.

3600 W. 80th Street
Bloomington, MN 55431
(612) 893-6915   Fax—(612) 896-3479

Search firm. Permanent placement of engineers in electrical/process controls, mechanical design, chemical, software applications, business information systems. Fax resume; follow up by phone. No applicant fees.

FINANCIAL INSTITUTION PERSONNEL SERVICES

1821 University Avenue, Suite S-252
St. Paul, MN 55104
(612) 647-1321   Fax—(612) 649-3165

Search firm, temp-to-perm opportunities. Serves all levels of staffing in finance and banking industry. Call for appointment. No fees to applicant.

FLATLEY SERVICES

Four metro locations, Le Sueur and Mankato. Call for locations.

3600 W. 80th St., Suite 535
Bloomington, MN 55431
(612) 896-3435   Fax—(612) 896-3477
Internet address: http://www.flatley.com
E-mail: inquiry@flatley.com

Contract and permanent placement services with diverse opportunities for technical, para-technical, software, personnel, law, records management.

GEORGE KONIK ASSOCIATES, INC.

7242 Metro Blvd.
Minneapolis, MN 55439
(612) 835-5550   Fax—(612) 835-7294

Contract and permanent employment service. Short and long-term engineering assignments for drafters, designers, engineers, programmers and project engineers. Mail resume; follow up by phone. No applicant fees.

H. L. YOH COMPANY

2626 E. 82nd St., Suite 355
Bloomington, MN 55425
(612) 854-2400   Fax—(612) 854-0512
Internet address: yohmpls@skypoint.com

Contract and permanent employment for experienced technical personnel in engineering, electronics, manufacturing and architecture. Mail resume.

H R SERVICES

3030 Harbor Lane, Suite 200-F
Plymouth, MN 55447
(612) 559-8841

Search firm. Mid- and upper management positions in engineering, industrial and technical manufacturing. Mail resume. No applicant fees.

HAYDEN AND ASSOCIATES

7825 Washington Avenue So., Suite 120
Bloomington, MN 55439
(612) 941-6300   Fax—(612) 941-9602
E-mail: hayden@usinternet.com

Search firm. Placement of experienced personnel in marketing, sales, MIS, engineering, accounting, management and computers. Also offers contract positions in information services. Fax or mail resume. No applicant fees.

HEALTHCARE RECRUITERS OF MINNESOTA

6442 City West Parkway, Suite 303
Eden Prairie, MN 55344
(612) 942-5424   Fax—(612) 942-5452

Search firm. Specializes in national healthcare recruiting for executive level management, sales, marketing, technical personnel in medical field; nurses at management level and physicians. Mail resume; follow up by phone. No applicant fees.

HENNEPIN COUNTY BAR ASSOCIATION PLACEMENT SERVICE

514 Nicollet Mall, Suite 350
Minneapolis, MN 55402
(612) 340-0022   Fax—(612) 340-9518

Search firm. Specializes in part-time, full-time and temporary placement of support staff in legal professions. Call for information or appointment. No fees to applicant.

HUMAN RESOURCES PERSONNEL SERVICES

6800 France Avenue South
Edina, MN 55435
(612) 929-3000   Fax—(612) 927-4313

Search firm. Specializes in permanent and temporary staffing in human resources. Positions served include management, generalists, compensation and benefits specialists, support staff. Fax resume; follow up by phone. No fees to applicant.

INSURANCE NETWORK GROUP

17750 State Highway 7
Minnetonka, MN 55345
(612) 470-6617

Search and temp firm. Specializes in permanent and temporary staffing for a broad variety of positions in the insurance industry. Also affiliated with a national network of recruiters. Call for appointment. No fees to applicant.

KELLY TEMPORARY SERVICES—ENCORE

3033 Campus Drive, Suite 430
Plymouth, MN 55441
(612) 553-1160   Fax—(612) 553-1220

Specializes in temp, temp-to-perm and permanent placements of mature workers in various industries. Positions for clerical, marketing, professional, technical, engineering, accounting personnel. Call for appointment. No applicant fees.

KREOFSKY AND ASSOCIATES

8400 Normandale Lake Blvd., Suite 920
Bloomington, MN 55437
(612) 921-8820   Fax—(612) 921-8821

Search firm. Specializes in computer sales and technical pre-sales personnel. Mail resume; follow up by phone. Fees paid by employer.

LEE MARSH AND ASSOCIATES

202N One Appletree Square
Bloomington, MN 55425
(612) 854-6811   Fax—(612) 452-9051
E-mail: marsh042@gold.tc.umn.edu

Search firm. Permanent placement of experienced workers through mid-management in the software engineering industry. Fax resume; follow up by phone. Fees paid by employer.

MACTEMPS

1611 W. County Road B, Suite 102
Roseville, MN 55113
(800) 622-8367   Fax—(612) 633-3206
Internet address: mactemps.com/minneapolis.html
E-mail: pdejaggw@mactemps.com

Temp, temp-to-perm and permanent placements for personnel at all levels with experience in desktop publishing, graphic design, multimedia, database design, word processing, art direction. No applicant fees.

MANAGEMENT RECRUITERS OF CHANHASSEN

80 W. 78th Street, Suite 230
Chanhassen, MN 55317-9705
(612) 937-9693   Fax—(612) 937-9697

Search firm. Permanent and interim placements for MIS, engineers, software developers, technical and management personnel in diverse industries. Fax resume; follow up by phone. Fees paid by employer.

MARY ERICKSON & ASSOCIATES

8300 Norman Center Drive, Suite 545
Minneapolis, MN 55437
(612) 893-1010   Fax—(612) 893-0130

Search firm. Industry generalist specializes in executive search only at senior level. Mail resume; follow up by phone. Fees paid by employer.

MASTERSON PERSONNEL INC.

5775 Wayzata Blvd., Suite 995
St. Louis Park, MN 55416
(612) 542-9300   Fax—(612) 542-3143

Employment agency. Permanent, temporary and contract positions in data processing and office services. Call for appointment or information. Fees paid by employer.

MEDSEARCH CORP.

Southdale Medical Center
6545 France Ave. So.
Edina, MN 55435
(612) 926-6584   Fax—(612) 926-7584

Employment agency. Permanent and temporary placements in all areas of medical field. Positions for support staff, executives and physicians. Fax or mail resume; follow up by phone. Fees paid by employer.

METRO HOSPITALITY CONSULTANTS

9448 Lyndale Avenue South, Suite 223
Bloomington, MN 55420
(612) 884-4299   Fax—(612) 884-4395

Employment agency. Specializes in permanent positions in hospitality industry including operations management. Mail resume; follow up by phone. No fees to applicant.

METRO MEDICAL PLACEMENT

Opus Center, Suite 105
9900 Bren Road East
Minnetonka, MN 55343
(612) 932-9933   Fax—(612) 932-0099

Search firm. Specializes in placement of medical personnel and support staff from entry level to executive positions. Call for appointment. Fees paid by employer.

NATIONAL ENGINEERING RESOURCES, INC.

6200 Shingle Creek Parkway, Suite 160
Brooklyn Center, MN 55430
(612) 561-7610   (800) 665-7610   Fax—(612) 561-7675
E-mail: dadelman@interserv.com

Contract and direct placement service. Specializes in nationwide placements of engineering, technical and scientific personnel. Mail or fax resume; follow up by phone. No fees to applicants.

PFAFFLY PERSONNEL RESOURCES, INC.

3055 Old Hwy. 8
Minneapolis, MN 55418
(612) 782-2445   (800) 780-2087   Fax—(612) 782-9097

Employment agency. Permanent and some temporary placements of experienced medical personnel through upper level management. Call for appointment. Fees paid by employer.

PINNACLE SEARCH LTD.

2500 W. County Road 42
Burnsville, MN 55337
(612) 894-7700   Fax—(612) 894-0453

Search firm and employment service. Specializes in permanent placement of mid-management positions in the paper, printing and packaging industries. Call for appointment. Fees paid by employer.

PROFESSIONAL ALTERNATIVES

601 Lakeshore Parkway, Suite 1050
Minneapolis, MN 55305-5219
(612) 975-9200   Fax—(612) 975-9296

Search firm and employment service. Specializes in temp-to-perm and some permanent placements in human resources, marketing, finance and other areas. Mail resume; follow-up by phone, or call for information. Fees paid by employer.

PROGRAMMING ALTERNATIVES INC.

6750 France Ave. So.
Edina, MN 55435
(612) 922-1103   Fax—(612) 922-3726

Contractual, consulting and permanent placement of experienced data processing and engineering professionals including programmers, analysts and project leaders. Call for information or appointment. No fees to applicant.

RAMSEY COUNTY BAR ASSO. PLACEMENT SERVICE

(612) 222-7301   Fax—(612) 223-8344

Search firm. Specializes in temporary and permanent placements for legal support staff. Opportunities for legal secretaries, legal assistants, receptionists and file clerks. Call for appointment. Fees paid by employer.

RETIREMENT ENTERPRISES

33 W. 65th St., Suite 10
Minneapolis, MN 55423
(612) 869-3301   Fax—(612) 869-8702

Temp, permanent and management/project consulting opportunities. Specializes in serving mature workers. Assignments include clerical, engineering, financial, in-store demonstrations and merchandising, light industrial and marketing. Call for appointment. No applicant fees.

ROBERT HALF INTERNATIONAL INC.

Call for locations in Bloomington, Plymouth and St. Paul.

2850 IDS Center
80 So. 8th Street
Minneapolis, MN 55402
(612) 339-9001   Fax—(612) 349-6769

Search firm. Permanent, temp and contract employment opportunities for financial execs, accountants, bookkeepers, information systems professionals. Mail resume; follow up by phone. No fees to applicant.

ROTH YOUNG EXECUTIVE RECRUITERS

4620 W. 77th Street, Suite 290
Minneapolis, MN 55435
(612) 831-6655   Fax—(612) 831-7413

Search firm. Recruitment of mid- to senior management in hotel and restaurant industries, food manufacturing, sales, retailing, supermarket and food wholesalers, health care. Mail resume; follow up by phone. No applicant fees.

SALES CONSULTANTS OF MINNEAPOLIS

7550 France Ave., Suite 180
Minneapolis, MN 55435
(612) 830-1420   Fax—(612) 893-9254

Search firm. Recruits for sales, sales management, and marketing personnel. Call for appointment. Fees paid by employer.

SALES SEARCH

8100 Mitchell Road
Eden Prairie, MN 55344
(612) 937-5429
Fax—(612) 937-6791

Search firm. Recruits for sales personnel at all levels, entry level through upper management in all industries. Fax or mail resume; follow-up by phone. Fees paid by employer.

SATHE & ASSOCIATES

5821 Cedar Lake Road
Minneapolis, MN 55416
(612) 546-2100
Fax—(612) 546-6930

Retainer search firm. Industry generalists with emphasis in senior management. Mail resume and cover letter. Fees paid by employer.

SENIOR DESIGN CORPORATION

7600 Parklawn Avenue
Edina, MN 55435
(612) 831-0111   Fax—(612) 831-0494

Contract employment service. Specializes in placement of technical professionals such as engineers, drafters, computer specialists and office support. Mail resume; follow up by phone. No fees to applicant.

SNELLING SEARCH

2665 Long Lake Rd., Suite 170
Roseville, MN 55113
(612) 631-3040   Fax—(612) 631-1455

Search firm. Recruits for permanent placements in engineering, IS, accounting and finance personnel. Mail resume; follow up by phone. Fees paid by employer.

SOURCE SERVICES

8500 Normandale Lake Blvd., Suite 2160
Bloomington, MN 55437
(612) 835-5100   Fax—(612) 835-1548
Internet address: http://www.sourcesvc.com
E-mail: srcmn@dice.com

Search firm. Permanent and contract positions for experienced personnel in computers, finance, accounting. Call for appointment. No applicant fees.

SOURCE TECH CORPORATION

7600 Parklawn Ave., Suite 204
Edina, MN 55435
(612) 831-8210
Fax—(612) 831-0494

Contract employment service. Engineering, drafting and technical positions. Mail or fax resume; follow up by phone. No applicant fees.

ST. CROIX TECHNICAL

8300 Norman Center Dr., Suite 890
Bloomington, MN 55437
(612) 832-8390   Fax—(612) 832-8366
E-mail: sct-is@ix.netcom.com

Contract employment service. Positions in engineering and manufacturing at all levels. Positions for programmers, drafters, engineers, designers and technicians. Mail or fax resume; follow up by phone. No applicant fees.

STROM ENGINEERING CORPORATION

10505 Wayzata Blvd.
Minnetonka, MN 55305
(612) 544-8644   (800) 205-8732   Fax—(612) 544-2451

Contract engineering service. Recruits engineering, drafting, design, technical writing, CAD personnel. Locations nationwide. Mail or fax resume; follow up by phone. No applicant fees.

SUPERIOR SENIOR SERVICES, INC.

2401-1/2 Central Ave. N.E.
Minneapolis, MN 55418
(612) 789-1616   Fax—(612) 789-0803

Temporary employment service. Specializes in placement of active seniors in positions such as light assembly, clerical, engineering, accounting and professional services. Four Twin Cities locations. Call for appointment. No fees to applicant.

T.H. HUNTER, INC.

526 Nicollet Mall, Suite 310
Minneapolis, MN 55402
(612) 339-0530   Fax—(612) 338-4757

Search firm. Generalists with emphasis in banking, engineering, data processing, marketing, medical, finance, insurance. Most positions are mid-management; some at senior level. Call for appointment. No applicant fees.

TAD RESOURCES INTERNATIONAL INC.

4820 W. 77th St., Suite 207
Edina, MN 55435
(612) 832-5443   Fax—(612) 832-9865

Contract and permanent employment for technical engineering personnel. Mail resume. No fees to applicant.

TECHPOWER, INC.

4510 W. 77th Street
Edina, MN 55435
(612) 831-7444   Fax—(612) 831-8621

Internet address: http://www.techpowerjobs.com
E-mail: hrdept@techpowerjobs.com

Contract placements in engineering and telecommunications for project engineers, programmers. Mail/fax resume. No applicant fees.

THE ESQUIRE GROUP

430 First Ave. No., Suite 630
Minneapolis, MN 55401
(612) 340-9068   (800) 755-7779   Fax—(612) 340-1218

Search firm. Specializes in permanent and temporary placements of all levels of attorneys, paralegals and legal assistants. Call for appointment. Fees paid by employer. Also offers career coaching services for attorneys.

THE NYCOR GROUP

4930 W. 77th St., Suite 300
Minneapolis, MN 55435
(612) 831-6444   Fax—(612) 835-2883

Internet address: http://www.nycor.com
E-mail: jobs@nycor.com

Contract engineering and executive search in all engineering disciplines. Specializes in placement of software, electrical, bio-medical, mechanical, engineering personnel. Call for information. Fees paid by employer.

THE RECRUITING GROUP

5354 Parkdale Dr., Suite 104
Minneapolis, MN 55416
(612) 544-8550   Fax—(612) 546-2806

Search firm. Permanent, contract and temporary placements for mid- to upper management in various industries. Fax or mail resume; follow up by phone. Fees paid by employer.

THOMAS MOORE, INC.

608 2nd Ave. So.
Minneapolis, MN 55402
(612) 338-4884   Fax—(612) 338-6506

Employment agency. Permanent and temporary placements of entry level to management positions in accounting. Call for appointment. Fees paid by employer.

WESTERN TECHNICAL SERVICES

3601 Minnesota Drive, Suite 500
Bloomington, MN 55435
(612) 835-4743   Fax—(612) 835-5419
E-mail: 102677.1316@compuserve.com

Contract employment service. Temporary and temp-to-perm placements: PC help desk/tech support, networking, engineers, technicians, programmers, technical writers, drafters, illustrators. Mail or fax resume; follow up by phone. No applicant fees.

WHITNEY & ASSOCIATES, INC.

920 Second Ave. So., Suite 625
Minneapolis, MN 55402-4035
(612) 338-5600   Fax—(612) 349-6129

Accounting search firm. Specializes in executive, management and staff personnel in accounting, bookkeeping and finance. Mail resume. No fees to applicant.

AAA EMPLOYMENT AGENCY OF DULUTH

2631 W. Superior Street, Suite 102
Duluth, MN 55806
(218) 727-8810   Fax—(218) 727-8830

Employment agency. Permanent placement at all levels in non-government types of positions. Call for appointment. Fees paid, upon placement, by job seeker and some employers.

ACTION-PLUS TEMPORARY SERVICE, INC.

141 E. Broadway
Monticello, MN 55362
(612) 295-4005   Fax—(612) 295-6240

Temporary employment service. Entry level positions in manufacturing, food production and other industries. Call to schedule an appointment. No fees to applicant.

DELACORE RESOURCES

101 Park Place, Suite 206
Hutchinson, MN 55350
(320) 587-4420   (800) 967-2711   Fax—(320) 587-7252
E-mail: delacore@hutchtel.net

Search firm. Specializes in permanent placements for personnel in healthcare positions including physicians, CRNAs, physical therapists and others. Call or mail resume. Fees paid by employer.

EXPRESS PERSONNEL SERVICES

Call for locations in Albert Lea, Mankato, Owatonna, Red Wing, Rochester, St. Cloud and Winona.

(800) 331-0853   Fax—(507) 285-1830

Provides permanent, temp, contract and temp-to-perm placement services for clerical, light industrial and technical personnel. Call for appointment. Fees paid by employer.

GIBBS TEMPORARY EMPLOYMENT SERVICE
1915 Hwy. 52 No., Suite 222-C
Rochester, MN 55901
(507) 288-3623   Fax—(507) 289-3345

Temporary employment service. Specializes in placements for entry level personnel in variety of industries. Call to schedule an appointment. No fees to applicant.

KELLY TEMPORARY SERVICES—ROCHESTER
3800 Hwy. 52 No., Suite 130
Rochester, MN 55901
(507) 282-1584   (800) 448-8908   Fax—(507) 282-2415

Temporary employment service. Specializes in temporary staffing at all levels in manufacturing, health care and medical industries. Call for appointment. No fees to applicant.

KELLY TEMPORARY SERVICES—ST. CLOUD
1010 W. St. Germain, Suite 400
St. Cloud, MN 56301
(320) 253-7430   (800) 447-6447
Fax—(320) 253-3913

Temporary employment service. Positions for light industrial, secretarial, sales promotion, data entry personnel. Call for appointment. Fees paid by employer.

LEIDERS EMPLOYMENT SERVICE
210 First Ave. S.W., Suite 429
Rochester, MN 55902
(507) 285-1425   Fax—(507) 285-1428

Employment agency. Provides career placements at all levels in diverse industries. Permanent and temporary positions. Call for appointment. Fees paid by employer.

GREATER MINNESOTA

McGLADREY AND PULLEN, LLP

700 Missabe Bldg.
Duluth, MN 55802
(218) 727-5025   Fax—(218) 727-1438

Search firm. Permanent, temp and temp-to-perm placements of upper and mid-management personnel in diverse industries. Call for appointment. Fees paid by employer.

MANAGEMENT RECRUITERS OF ROCHESTER

1903 So. Broadway
Rochester, MN 55904
(507) 282-2400   Fax—(507) 282-1308

Search firm. Permanent, temp-to-hire and temporary executive positions for information systems personnel. Fax or mail resume, or call for appointment. Fees paid by employer.

MANPOWER TEMPORARY SERVICES

940 37th St. N.W.   920 Hoffman Drive
Rochester, MN 55901   Owatonna, MN 55060
(507) 285-0710   (507) 451-3404   (800) 638-9889

Temporary employment service. Specializes in positions at all levels in variety of industries. Call for appointment. No fees to applicant.

MIDTOWN STAFFING SERVICES

217 Plum Street
Red Wing, MN 55066
(612) 388-2261   (800) 829-5354
Fax—(612) 388-5549

Employment agency. Permanent and temporary positions from entry level to management in diverse industries. Call to schedule an appointment. Fees paid by employer.

OLSTEN STAFFING SERVICES
110 Fitger Complex, 600 E. Superior Street
Duluth, MN 55802
(218) 720-3265   Fax—(218) 720-3325

Search firm. Permanent, contract and temporary positions in diverse industries. Call for appointment. Fees paid by employer.

PRO STAFF PERSONNEL
101 7th Avenue So., Suite 100
St. Cloud, MN 56301
(320) 656-9777   (800) 656-5405   Fax—(320) 656-9776

Temporary employment service. Positions in general clerical and light industrial. Call for appointment. Fees paid by employer.

QUALITY TEMP / QUALITY STAFFING SOLUTIONS
Call for additional locations in Alexandria, Hutchinson, Monticello, New Ulm, Owatonna and Red Wing.

1600 Madison Ave., Suite 108
Mankato, MN 56001
(507) 387-5009

15 N. Sixth Ave., Suite D
St. Cloud, MN 56303
(320) 259-4004

Temporary industrial employment. Call for appointment. No fees to applicant.

RWJ AND ASSOCIATES
2360 No. Broadway
Rochester, MN 55906
(507) 285-9270
(800) 331-0853
Fax—(507) 285-1830

812 S. Elm Street
Owatonna, MN 55060
(507) 455-3002
Fax—(507) 455-0271

Search firm. Specializes in a variety of positions for mid- to upper management. Mail resume; follow up by phone. No applicant fees.

GREATER MINNESOTA

SEARCH RESOURCES, INC.

214 First Ave. N.W.
Grand Rapids, MN 55744
(218) 326-9461   Fax—(218) 326-9463

Temporary, contract and permanent placements in manufacturing industry. Call for appointment. Fees paid by employer.

SUTHERS AND ASSOCIATES

P.O. Box 981
Monticello, MN 55362
(612) 878-2079   Fax—(612) 878-2547

Search firm. Specializes in food and manufacturing industry. Permanent placements in technical sales, marketing, R & D, quality, engineering, general management. Mail or fax resume; follow up by phone. Fees paid by employer.

TECHNICAL CAREER PLACEMENTS INC.

1915 Highway 52 No., Suite 222-C
Rochester, MN 55901
(507) 288-3623   Fax—(507) 289-3345

Search firm. Permanent and contract placements of mid- to upper managers in engineering, hardware/software engineers and computer programmers. Mail or fax resume; or call for appointment. Generally fees paid by employer.

THE WORK CONNECTION

2719 Division Street West, Suite 4
St. Cloud, MN 56301
(320) 259-9675

Temporary employment service. General, industrial and clerical positions for entry through senior level personnel. Drop in to complete an application. Applications kept on file one year. Fees paid by employer.

RESUME

DATABASES

Resume databases offer another way to bring employers and job seekers together to hire and be hired. Resume database services collect resumes from job seekers then post them for employers or recruiters to review. Some organizations also actively match job seekers to open positions.

◆ To post your resume with a database service, submit a readable copy of your resume by mail, E-mail, fax or modem. Some services accept only resumes submitted electronically, online or on disk, and charge an additional fee to process paper resumes. Others don't accept resumes at all. Instead, job seekers are asked to complete a "profile" application.

◆ After you submit your resume, your work is done. The sponsoring organization will store your resume, typically in a computer database. Some databases are privately maintained but many are open to the public via the Internet or online bulletin board system.

◆ Some resume databases charge a fee. If you're willing to pay for this service, understand what you'll get for your money. Find out how long the organization has been in business. Ask about the placement success of past users. Which employers have access to your resume? How long will your resume remain in the system?

◆ Additional resume database sources: Many career-related Internet sites also maintain resume databases open to the public. See listings beginning on page 98. Some professional associations and networking groups offer job matching or resume database services to members. See page 228.

ARMY EMPLOYER NETWORK

331 Second Ave. So., Room 450
Minneapolis, MN 55401-2253
(612) 339-3914

Resume database and job matching service targeted to downsized army personnel. Worldwide job openings with employers interested in hiring army alumni. Call for information. Free.

CORSEARCH

1 Pierce Place, Suite 300
Itasca, IL 60143
(708) 250-8667   (800) 323-1352   Fax—(708) 250-7362
Internet address: http://www.cors.com
E-mail: dgeron@interaccess.com

Resume database and job matching service targeted to job seekers worldwide. Resumes remain on file indefinitely. Call for fee information.

CENTER FOR CAREER CHANGE JOB REFERRAL SERVICE
Division of Metropolitan Senior Federation

1885 University Avenue
St. Paul, MN 55104
(612) 645-0261   (800) 365-8765   Fax—(612) 641-8969

Job referral service. Matches older workers, ages 55 and up, by skills and experience to listed job openings. Call for information. No charge.

ELECTRONIC JOB MATCHING

1915 No. Dale Mabry Highway, Suite 307
Tampa, FL 33607
(813) 879-4100

Resume database and job matching service targeted to job seekers nationwide in all professions except medical. Resumes remain on file for four months. Call for information. No charge.

JOB BANK USA

1420 Spring Hill Road, Suite 480
McLean, VA 22102
(800) 296-1872

Resume database serving all professions, crafts and trades nationwide. Resumes remain on file for one year. Call to enroll. Fee, $96.

MEPS

Minnesota Educators' Placement Service
P.O. Box 526, Stillwater, MN 55082
Phone/Fax—(612) 430-2005

Job vacancy and matching service targeted to Minnesota teachers, administrators and educators, elementary through post-secondary. Vacancy list mailed bi-weekly. Call or write for information and fees.

MINNESOTA SKILLSNET

Minnesota Department of Economic Security
444 Cedar St., 610 Piper Jaffray Plaza
St. Paul, MN 55101
(612) 282-6680   Fax—(612) 296-2732
Internet address: http://mnjobsearch.org/js/killsnt.htm

Resume database targeted to Minnesota job seekers. Resumes are scanned into an electronic database that identifies education, experience and up to 80 skills. Applicants are then screened against job openings listed with Job Service. Mail, fax or drop off resume at local Job Service office. No charge.

NATIONAL RESUME BANK

3637 4th Street No., Suite 330
St. Petersburg, FL 33704
(813) 896-3694

Resume database and job matching service for job seekers nationwide. Resumes remain on file indefinitely. Call for information. One time fee, $40.

RESUME-ON-FILE
Association Trends Magazine

7910 Woodmont Ave., Suite 1150, Bethesda, MD 20814
(301) 652-8666   Fax—(301) 656-8654
E-mail: 75601.3370@Compuserve.com

Resume database targeted to entry-level through senior executives seeking jobs with associations nationwide. Applicant prepares 30-word classified ad and submits 10 resumes. Fees, $63 every 3 weeks.

SKILLSEARCH

3354 Perimeter Hill Dr., Suite 235, Nashville, TN 37211
(800) 252-5665   Fax—(615) 834-9453
Internet address: http://www.internet_is.com/skillsearch//

Resume database for job seekers in white-collar and technical positions. Resumes remain on file one year. Fees, $65 first year/$15 thereafter.

THE CHRISTIAN PLACEMENT NETWORK

19303 Freemont Ave. No., Seattle, WA 98133-9906
(206) 546-7330   (800) 251-7740
Internet address: http.\\www.halcyon.com\ico\

Resume database and job matching service. Positions with non-profit Christian organizations worldwide. Fees, $42.50 for 3 months.

TIES
Technology Information Educational Services
1925 W. County Road B2, Roseville, MN 55113
Applicant Search Info—(612) 638-2395   Fax—(612) 631-7519
Internet address: http://www.ties.k12.mn.us/depts/appsearch
E-mail: applicant.search@ties.k12.mn.us

Job matching service for educational professionals, K-12, including teachers and administrators. Applicant's profile is matched to the hiring needs of participating employers and school districts. Call for information and fees.

RECRUITMENT
PUBLICATIONS

If you're intent on tracking down job openings, don't overlook recruitment publications. These useful periodicals ranging from chatty newsletters to slick, career-track magazines publish current job vacancies. One may be just the ticket to your next job.

◆ Though some recruitment publications offer general employment opportunities, most serve a specific niche. Some focus on positions in a particular field, industry or profession. Others specialize in jobs offered by the public or non-profit sector. Still others report openings by level of work experience: senior management, recent college graduates, etc.

◆ Few publications exclusively list Minnesota job opportunities. It's more common to find publications with a nationwide circulation that list openings throughout the country. Therefore, it you have no plans to relocate, these resources may have limited appeal.

◆ Don't look for too many recruitment publications at area newsstands. Most are available only by subscription. Subscriptions generally are short-term but it's a good idea to request a free sample before subscribing.

◆ Three good books can help you track down hard-to-find recruitment publications including many sponsored by associations: *Professional's Job Finder, Non Profit Job Finder* and *Government Job Finder,* all published by Planning/Communications, (800) 829-5220.

ACCESS: NETWORKING IN THE PUBLIC INTEREST

1001 Connecticut Ave. N.W., Suite 838
Washington, D.C. 20036
(202) 785-4233   Fax—(202) 785-4212

Monthly tabloid with editorial articles and job vacancies, entry-level through senior executive, at non-profit organizations. Subscription, $25 for 3 issues; 39 for 6 issues. Call or write for information.

AFFIRMATIVE ACTION REGISTER

8356 Olive Blvd.
St. Louis, MO 63132
(800) 537-0655   Fax—(314) 997-1788

Free monthly publication directed to females, minorities, veterans, disabled. About 150 manager/professional job vacancies per issue at colleges, universities, government, hospitals nationwide. Call to be added to mailing list.

AIR JOBS DIGEST

7800 Airpark Road, Suite 23
Gaithersburg, MD 20879
(800) 247-5627   Fax—(301) 990-8484

Monthly tabloid with 500-1,000 worldwide job opportunities in aviation, aerospace, and space industries. Positions for pilots, mechanics, technicians, flight attendants, engineers, management. Subscription, $49 for 3 issues; $69 for 6 issues.

AMERICAN EMPLOYMENT WEEKLY

P.O. Box 11268
South Bend, IN 46634
(219) 277-3408   Fax—(219) 277-1141

Weekly tabloid with 2,000 jobs in accounting, banking, finance, engineering, human resources, insurance, management, manufacturing, marketing, sales, data processing—all levels through management. Subscription, $3.50 for sample issue; $44 for 13 issues. Call or write for information.

ARTJOB

236 Montezuma Ave.
Santa Fe, NM 87501
(505) 982-0532   Fax—(505) 983-3732
Internet address: http://www.webart.com/artjob/

Bi-weekly arts employment publication. Subscription, $40 for 12 issues. Sample issue on request.

CAREER FOCUS

New Mexico State University, Placement & Career Services
P.O. Box 30001, Dept. 3509
Las Cruces, NM 88003-8001
(505) 646-1631   Fax—(505) 646-5421

Bi-weekly tabloid with about 200 jobs nationwide in liberal arts, business, agriculture, engineering, technical fields, education, government. Subscription, $12.60/six months. Sample issue on request. Call or write for information.

CAREERS AND THE DISABLED

1160 E. Jericho Turnpike, Suite 200
Huntington, NY 11743
(516) 421-9402   Fax—(516) 421-0359

Quarterly magazine with 50+ jobs nationwide in the private sector. Includes braille section. Pre-paid subscription, $10 for 4 issues; $15 per year on computer disk. Call or write for information.

CLASSIFACTS

2821 So. Parker Rd., #305
Aurora, CO 80014
(303) 745-1011   (800) 234-1254   Fax—(303) 745-1122
Internet address: http://www.classifacts.com

Weekly report based on search of 45 Sunday newspapers using customer-defined job titles and geographic locations. Maximum 125 listings per week. Subscription, $55.80 for four reports, includes overnight delivery.

CONTRACT EMPLOYMENT WEEKLY

P.O. Box 97000

Kirkland, WA 98083-9700

(206) 823-2222   Fax—(206) 821-0942

Internet address: http://www.ceweekly.com

Weekly newsletter includes approximately 4,000-5,000 contract technical jobs, nationwide and overseas. Call or write for information. Subscription rate, $6, single issue; $18 for 5 issues; $30 for 12 issues.

CURRENT JOBS FOR GRADUATES

P.O. Box 3505

McLean, Virginia 22103

(703) 506-4400

National employment bulletin for liberal arts professions. Published twice monthly. Each issue lists approximately 185-200 jobs for early career positions. Subscription, $25 for 6 issues; $59 for 24 issues.

EMPLOYMENT REVIEW

1655 Palm Beach Lakes Blvd., Suite 600

West Palm Beach, FL 33401

(407) 686-6800   Fax—(407) 686-6796

Internet address: http://www.bestjobsusa.com

E-mail: recourse1@aol.com

Monthly tabloid with nationwide job listings for professional and high-tech. Editorial support articles. About 200 listings in 80 pages. Available at local newsstands. Subscription, $13.95 for 6 issues; $24.95 for 12 issues.

ENVIRONMENTAL CAREER OPPORTUNITIES

P.O. Box 560, Stanardsville, VA 22973

(804) 985-8627   Fax—(804) 985-2331

Bi-weekly magazine with 400 jobs in public/private sector of environmental field. Subscription, $29 for 4 issues; $49 for 8 issues. Sample on request.

ENVIRONMENTAL OPPORTUNITIES

P.O. Box 788
Walpole, NH 03608
(305) 866-0084   Fax—(305) 866-0091

Monthly newsletter. Listings for entry- to mid-level jobs in environmental field. Experience requirements range from 0-10 years. Includes seasonal positions and internships. Subscription, $26/6 issues; $47/12 issues.

EXEC-U-NET

25 Van Zant St.
Norwalk, CT 06855
(203) 851-5180   (800) 637-3126

Bi-weekly newsletter for senior execs with incomes over $70,000. About 300+ unadvertised positions in management, finance, sales, marketing, operations. Must join network designed to assist active career management. Membership, $110/3 months; $170/6 months. Call for information.

FEDERAL CAREER OPPORTUNITIES

P.O. Box 1059
Vienna, VA 22183-1059
(800) 822-5627   Fax—(703) 281-7639
Internet address: http://www/fedjobs.com

Each bi-weekly issue lists thousands of jobs at all agencies of federal government from GS-5 level to senior executive. Subscription, $39/6 issues; $77 for 12 issues. Also available on-line, $45/hour. Write or call to subscribe.

FEDERAL JOBS DIGEST

325 Pennsylvania Ave. S.E.
Washington, DC 20003
(800) 824-5000   Fax—(914) 762-5695

Bi-weekly tabloid lists federal jobs nationwide. Also offers Federal Job Matching Service at additional fee, matching applicants to suitable federal careers. Call or write to subscribe. $34 for 6 issues.

INTERNATIONAL CAREER EMPLOYMENT OPPORTUNITIES

Route 2, Box 305, Stanardsville, VA 22973

(804) 985-6444   Fax—(804) 985-6828

Bi-weekly magazine lists 600-700 nationwide and overseas jobs in foreign policy, education, communication, trade/finance, environmental programs. Subscription, $29 for 4 issues; $49 for 8 issues. Free issue upon request.

INTERNATIONAL EMPLOYMENT GAZETTE

220 No. Main St., Suite 100

Greenville, SC 29601

(800) 882-9188   Fax—(864) 235-3369

E-mail: Intljobs@aol.com

Bi-weekly 64-page magazine with over 400 overseas job opportunities. Primarily white-collar positions. Call for informational brochure. Available at selected local bookstores. Subscription, $35 for 6 issues.

JOB INFORMATION LETTER

National Association of Government Communicators

669 South Washington St.

Alexandria, VA 22314

(703) 519-3902   Fax—(703) 519-7732

Bi-weekly newsletter with approximately 500 communications positions with federal government and non-government employers in U.S. Free to members; $50 per year/non-members. Call or write for sample.

JOB OPPORTUNITIES FOR THE BLIND

National Federation of the Blind

1800 Johnson St.

Baltimore, MD 21230

(410) 659-9314   (800) 638-7518

Bi-monthly voice recorded bulletin. Twenty-minute tape lists 25-100 jobs in private sector. Call to order. Free to U.S. residents who are legally blind.

JOBS

345 Cedar St.
St. Paul, MN 55101
(612) 228-5288   (800) 950-9080   (800) 328-1478
Fax—(612) 228-5268
Internet address: http://www.pioneerplanet.com

Weekly tabloid lists approximately 3,500 job opportunities in all areas. Call to order print copy. Also available online. Free.

JOBS & EDUCATIONAL OPPORTUNITIES MAGAZINE

4445 West 77th St.
Minneapolis, MN 55435
(612) 835-4989   (800) 835-4989   Fax—(612) 835-0727
Fax—(800) 872-0727

Targeted to students and recent alumni. Quarterly magazine lists about 50 part-time and full-time entry level jobs. Available at University of Minnesota (Twin Cities only) drop spots. Free.

MINNESOTA CAREER OPPORTUNITIES
Minnesota Department of Employee Relations

200 C.O.B., 658 Cedar St.
St. Paul, MN 55155
(612) 296-2616

Bi-weekly pamphlet. Published by State of Minnesota. Lists 20-25 civil service jobs. Call for recorded instructions on how to receive publication.

NATIONAL AND FEDERAL LEGAL EMPLOYMENT REPORT

1010 Vermont Ave. N.W., Suite 408
Washington, D.C. 20005
(202) 393-3311   Fax—(202) 393-1553

Monthly newsletter. 500+ job vacancies in U.S. and abroad in law and law-related professions. Subscription, $69 for 6 issues; $39 for 3 issues.

NATIONAL BUSINESS EMPLOYMENT WEEKLY

P.O. Box 300
Princeton, NJ 08543
(800) 562-4868

Weekly tabloid published by Wall Street Journal includes ads for nationwide jobs plus articles on job-search strategy, franchise opportunities. Available at local newsstands. Subscription, $3.95 per single issue; $35 for 8 issues.

NATIONWIDE JOBS IN DIETETICS

P.O. Box 3537
Santa Monica, CA 90408-3537
(310) 453-5375
E-mail: cbcaesar@aol.com

Bi-weekly newsletter with 450 nationwide job opportunities for dietitians, nutritionists, food service professionals. Subscription, $25 for two issues; $42 for four issues. Free sample issue on request.

P R MARCOM JOBS NEWSLETTER SERIES

Mid-West Office, 500 No. Michigan Ave., #1920
Chicago, IL 60611
(312) 283-8455   (800) 874-8577

Bi-weekly newsletter with 100 nationwide job opportunities in advertising, marketing, public relations and journalism, plus internships, part-time and freelance work. Available by mail or fax. Subscription, $39 for two months. Sample issue on request.

PUBLIC SECTOR JOB BULLETIN

P.O. Box 1222
Newton, IA 50208-1222
(515) 791-9019   Fax—(515) 791-1005

Bi-weekly listing of job opportunities in city and county governments nationwide. Subscription rate, $22 for 26 issues; $14 for 13 issues. Free sample is available on request.

SOCIAL SERVICE JOBS

10 Angelica Drive
Framingham, MA 01701
(508) 626-8644   Fax—(508) 626-9389

Bi-weekly newsletter with listings for 150-170 current jobs in the social services, nationwide. Subscription rate, $42 for 6 issues; $59 for 12 issues. Free sample issue is available upon request.

TECHNICAL EMPLOYMENT

12416 Hymeadow Drive
Austin, TX 78750-1896
(800) 678-9724   (512) 250-8127   Fax—(512) 331-3900
Internet address: http://www.pcinews.com/pci
E-mail: editors@pcinews.com

Weekly magazine with over 200 job opportunities in contract technical employment. Subscription, $30 for 15 issues. Free sample on request.

THE INSIDER

P.O. Box 10129
Phoenix, AZ 85064
(800) 776-7877   Fax—(602) 955-3441

Twice monthly newsletter with approximately 75 job opportunities nationwide in the business aspect of the sports industry. Subscription rate, $99 for 12 issues; $149 for 24 issues.

THE JOB SEEKER

Route 2, Box 16
Warrens, WI 54666
(608) 378-4290
E-mail: bpottertjs@aol.com

Bi-weekly newsletter covers natural resources and environmental fields nationwide with 200 job vacancies per issue. Entry- through senior executive levels. Subscription, $19.50 for 6 issues. Call for sample.

THE NATIONAL AD SEARCH

P.O. Box 2083
Milwaukee, WI 53201
(800) 992-2832   Fax—(414) 351-0836

Weekly tabloid lists 2,400 nationwide job openings by career category, compiled from 75 major Sunday newspapers. Offers resume exchange service. Subscriptions start at $40 for 6 issues. Free sample on request.

THE POSITION REPORT

809 Ridge Road, Suite 206M
Wilmette, IL 60091
(708) 256-8826   (800) 962-4947   Fax—(708) 256-8937
BBS Data—(708) 256-8836

Weekly newsletter with over 500 nationwide jobs in law professions. Call to register or register online. Subscription, $43.50 for 4 issues.

THE POSITION REPORT II

Government Plus

809 Ridge Road, Suite 206M
Wilmette, IL 60091
(708) 256-8826   Fax—(708) 256-8937
BBS Data—(708) 256-8836

Weekly newsletter lists over 500 jobs with law firms, state, federal and local governments and non-attorney business related positions. Subscription, $43.50 for 4 issues.

TWIN CITIES EMPLOYMENT WEEKLY

10 So. 5th St., Suite 200
Minneapolis, MN 55408
(612) 321-7344   Fax—(612) 321-7350

Weekly recruitment newspaper with numerous current job openings. Free at metro locations.

FOR
WORKLIFE
ALTERNATIVES

- ◆ Self-Employment Resources
- ◆ Educational Centers
- ◆ Retirement Planning Services

O kay, so you're not exactly sure you want to plunge back into the same old job at a brand new company. Maybe you're bored with a dead-end position. Maybe you lost your job during the last corporate cut, and the possibilities of finding another one in your industry look pretty bleak. Maybe you opted for early retirement and can't wait to start a new mid-life career.

Maybe it's time to consider your options.

In this section, you'll encounter alternatives to re-entering the traditional job market: Resources for buying or starting a business; schools and training opportunities to broaden your knowledge or skills; retirement planning services to prepare you for a new stage in life.

For those with the luxury—or need—to explore career-related alternatives, here's where to look.

SELF EMPLOYMENT

RESOURCES

Unemployment produces entrepreneurs. At least that's what data by the Department of Labor reveals. One year after the last recession began in July of 1990, ranks of self-employed swelled to the highest level in 25 years. Some job-search consultants report that one in six of their clients goes solo after losing a job.

No surprise.

◆ To the victims of corporate downsizing or government cutbacks, business ownership promises perks: Control. Income potential. Challenge. Independence. Flexible hours. To name a few. So if you want your next boss to be *you*, your first job as CEO is to approach the task armed with as much information as possible.

◆ In Minnesota you can tap a variety of free or low-cost resources for entrepreneurs including consulting services, workshops and start-up kits. Libraries can help you track down potential competition or research an industry. Colleges, technical schools and community education departments offer small business education. There are even mentorship programs staffed by current or retired business owners familiar with specific businesses or industries.

◆ Interested in buying an existing business? Healthy businesses are not always publicly announced for sale. To seek out leads, consult business brokers, bankers, attorneys, accountants, sales reps, insurance agents, SBA liquidation officers, trade associations or newspaper ads.

AMERICAN INSTITUTE OF SMALL BUSINESS

7515 Wayzata Blvd., Suite 201
Minneapolis, MN 55426
(612) 545-7001   Fax—(612) 545-7020

Business publisher offers seminars and videos, software and books on topics that include starting and operating a business, advertising, marketing and more. Call for catalog. Seminar fees vary.

ARROWHEAD COMMUNITY ECONOMIC ASSISTANCE CORP.

702 Third Ave. South
Virginia, MN 55792-2797
(800) 662-5711   Fax—(218) 749-2912 ext. 287

Small business center helps with business plans, loan applications, operations management. Also offers workshops and counseling.

COUNCIL OF INDEPENDENT PROFESSIONAL CONSULTANTS

1711 W. County Rd. B, Suite 300N
Roseville, MN 55113
(612) 635-0306   Fax—(612) 635-0307

Targeted to consultants and independent professionals. Provides networking opportunities and informal advising for prospective consultants. Assistance with marketing, record-keeping, computers, promotions, accounts. Drop in or call for further information, meeting locations, schedules and dues. Dues, $100/year.

DAY WORKS

120 N.E. First Street
Rochester, MN 55906
(507) 281-6323   Fax—(507) 281-6605

Rents IBM and Macintosh laptop computers, modems and printers for business and other use. Overhead projection panel is also available that connects to computer for presentations.

FRANCHISE OPPORTUNITIES GUIDE

International Franchise Association

1350 New York Avenue N.W., Suite 900
Washington, DC 20005
(202) 628-8000
(800) 543-1038
Fax—(202) 628-0812

Targeted to prospective franchise owners. Publication includes national franchisors, costs and other details. Call for information or to order. Publication fee, $21.

HOMEBASED BUSINESS ASSOCIATION OF MINNESOTA

5115 Excelsior Blvd., Suite 211
St. Louis Park, MN 55416
(612) 361-3701
(800) 865-3486   Fax—(612) 930-0798
Internet address: www.bpsi.net\hbba
E-mail: mark@hbba.org

Targeted to new and experienced business owners, consultants and freelancers. Services include workshops and seminars, networking opportunities, newsletter and resource library. Assistance with developing contacts and promotion. Call for further information. Dues, $52/year; Non-member fees start at $10/meeting.

METROPOLITAN ECONOMIC DEVELOPMENT ASSOCIATION

2021 E. Hennepin Ave., Suite 370
Minneapolis, MN 55413
(612) 378-0361
Fax—(612) 378-9342

Open to African-Americans, Hispanics, Asians, Native Americans and other minorities. Offers business consulting, mentorship program and seminars. Call for appointment. Consulting is free.

MINNEAPOLIS / ST. PAUL MINORITY BUSINESS DEVELOPMENT CENTER

2021 E. Hennepin Ave., Suite LL35
Minneapolis, MN 55413
(612) 331-5576   Fax—(612) 331-1045

Open only to ethnic minorities who own/operate at least 51 percent of a business in the 10 county metro area. Offers individual counseling and assistance with business plan, loan applications, marketing, cash-flow management, operations management, market research and feasibility studies. Call for appointment. Consulting fees start at $10/hour. Sliding fee.

MINNESOTA TECHNOLOGY PROJECT OUTREACH

Teltech Resource Network

2850 Metro Drive
Minneapolis, MN 55425-1566
(612) 851-7750—Twin Cities
(800) 338-7005—Greater Minnesota

Business assistance program. Comprehensive service assisting state businesses with technology and scientific information available from University of Minnesota and other institutions. Also assists small and mid-sized businesses in finding technical and financial assistance. Provides referrals to state and national consultants, conducts business research and vendor/patent searches. Call for Minnesota locations.

MINNESOTA SMALL BUSINESS DEVELOPMENT CENTERS

Call for locations throughout Minnesota.

(612) 297-5771   (800) 657-3858—Greater Minnesota only
Fax—(612) 296-1290 Twin Cities only

Business assistance program for experienced or new entrepreneurs. Offices located throughout Minnesota are generally housed on college campuses. Services include one-to-one consulting on business plans, accounting, marketing, financing, loan preparation and operations management. Also offers workshops/seminars on specialized topics. Free.

NORTHEAST ENTREPRENEUR FUND, INC.

820 9th Avenue No.
Virginia, MN 55792
(218) 749-4191   Fax—(218) 741-4249

Offers workshops, business counseling. Loan program for startup and experienced business owners in Aitkin, Carlton, Cook, Itasca, Lake, St. Louis and Koochiching Counties. Call for information. Sliding Fee.

REGIONAL BUSINESS INCUBATORS

Business incubators provide office, warehouse or retail space at below-market rent, flexible leases, shared office services and free business advice.

TWIN CITIES

BBD Business and Technology Center, Minneapolis, (612) 378-1144
Corporate Visions, Empire Builder Center, St. Paul, (612) 223-8600
Franklin Business Center, Minneapolis, (612) 870-7555
Genesis Business Centers LTD, Columbia Heights, (612) 782-8576
Lowertown Business Center, St. Paul, (612) 291-8995
Minnesota Medical Enterprise Park, Coon Rapids, (612) 786-0869
St. Paul/Metro East Development Corp., St. Paul, (612) 266-6686
University of St. Thomas Enterprise Ctr., Chaska, (612) 448-8800
University Technology Center, Minneapolis, (612) 379-3800

GREATER MINNESOTA

Aitkin County Growth Center, Aitkin, (218) 927-2172
Breckenridge Business Center, Breckenridge, (218) 643-1431
Fairmont Development Center, Fairmont, (507) 238-9461
Henderson Business Center, Henderson, (507) 248-9664
Joint Economic Development Commission, Bemidji, (218) 751-6529
Leech Lake Tribal Council, Cass Lake, (218) 335-8330
Mankato Manufacturing Incubator, Mankato, (507) 387-8686
Owatonna Incubator Inc., Owatonna, (507) 451-0517
St. Cloud Business Center, St. Cloud, (320) 259-4000

REGIONAL DEVELOPMENT COMMISSIONS

Small business assistance centers offer workshops, publications, networking opportunities, revolving loan fund for startup and experienced business owners. Call for appointment. Free.

ARROWHEAD
330 Canal Park Drive
Duluth, MN 55802
(218) 722-5545
(800) 232-0707

CENTRAL
611 Iowa Avenue
Staples, MN 56479
(218) 894-3233
Fax—(218) 894-1328

EAST CENTRAL
P.O. Box 147
Mora, MN 55051
(320) 679-4065
Fax—(320) 679-4120

HEADWATERS
403 Fourth St. N.W.
P.O. Box 906
Bemidji, MN 56601
(218) 751-3108
Fax—(218) 751-3695

MID-MINNESOTA
333 West Sixth St.
Willmar, MN 56201
(320) 235-8504
Fax—(320) 235-4329

NORTHWEST
1155 Main, Suite 1
Warren, MN 56762
(218) 745-6733
Fax—(218) 681-2670

REGION 9
410 Jackson St., P.O. Box 3367
Mankato, MN 56002
(507) 387-5643
(800) 450-5643

SOUTHWEST
2524 Broadway Ave.
P.O. Box 265
Slayton, MN 56172
(507) 836-8547

UPPER MINNESOTA VALLEY
323 W. Schlieman Avenue
Appleton, MN 56206
(320) 289-1981
(800) 752-1983
Fax—(320) 289-1983

REGIONAL PUBLICATIONS

Several regional periodical publications can assist new and existing business owners. Most can be found in libraries or on local newsstands. To subscribe, call the numbers listed below.

CityBusiness
(612) 288-2100

Corporate Report Minnesota
(612) 338-4288

Twin Cities Business Monthly
(612) 339-7571

Minnesota Business Opportunities
(612) 844-0400

Minnesota Ventures
(612) 338-4288

Homebased & Small Business Network
(612) 689-1630

ST. CLOUD AREA ECONOMIC DEVELOPMENT PARTNERSHIP

St. Cloud Chamber of Commerce
30 Sixth Ave. South
St. Cloud, MN 56302
(320) 252-2177   (800) 523-0670   Fax—(320) 251-0081

Publishes "Getting Started in Business in the St. Cloud Area" which lists financing options, business start-up check list, sample business plan. $5.

SBA SMALL BUSINESS ANSWER DESK

U.S. Small Business Administration

(800) 827-5722

Business assistance helpline. Pre-recorded information on how to start a business and order SBA publications. Also offers option to speak directly to SBA counselor.

SCORE
Service Corps of Retired Executives

Business assistance program for new and existing business owners. Seminars cover SBA loan applications, financial statements, marketing plans, market research and more. Also offers free counseling by retired business people. Small fee for seminars.

NATIONAL SCORE OFFICE
409 Third St. S.W., Ste. 5900
Washington, DC 20024-3212
(800) 634-0245

ALBERT LEA
202 No. Broadway
Albert Lea, MN 56007
(507) 373-3939

ALEXANDRIA
Alexandria Technical College
RR 5, Box 199B
Alexandria, MN 56308
(320) 852-7752

AUSTIN
Chamber of Commerce
P.O. Box 894
Austin, MN 55912
(507) 437-4561

BURNSVILLE
101 Burnsville Pkwy., Ste. 150
Burnsville, MN 55337
(612) 898-5645

CAMBRIDGE
Chamber of Commerce
P.O. Box 343
Cambridge, MN 55008

FAIRMONT
Chamber of Commerce
206 No. State Street
Fairmont, MN 56031
(507) 235-5547

LONG PRAIRIE
Route 3, Box 6
Long Prairie, MN 56347
(320) 732-4172

MANKATO
Box 999
112 Riverfront Drive
Mankato, MN 56001
(507) 345-4519

MARSHALL
P.O. Box 352B
1210 East College Drive
Marshall, MN 56258
(507) 532-4484

MINNEAPOLIS
5217 Wayzata Blvd.
North Plaza Bldg., Suite 51
St. Louis Park, MN 55416
(612) 591-0539

OWATONNA
320 Hoffman Drive
Owatonna, MN 55060
(507) 451-7970

RED WING
2000 West Main Street, #324B
Red Wing, MN 55066
(612) 388-4079

ROCHESTER
Chamber of Commerce
220 So. Broadway, Suite 100
Rochester, MN 55904
(507) 288-1122

ST. CLOUD
Stearns Cty Nat'l Bank Bldg
4191 Second St. South
St. Cloud, MN 56301
(320) 255-4955

ST. PAUL
101 Norwest Center
55 E. Fifth St.
St. Paul, MN 55101
(612) 223-5010

WINONA
67 Main Street
Winona, MN 55987
(507) 452-2272

WORTHINGTON
1121 Third Ave.
Worthington, MN 56187
(507) 372-2919

SOUTHEASTERN MINNESOTA INITIATIVE FUND
540 West Hills Circle, Suite 201
Owatonna, MN 55060-4701
(507) 455-3215   Fax—(507) 455-2098

Networking and funding source for startup and experienced business owners. Workshops, assistance with loan applications. Free publications.

THE COLLABORATIVE
10 So. Fifth St., Suite 415
Minneapolis, MN 55402
(612) 338-3828   Fax—(612) 338-1876

Information and networking for Minnesota companies. Meetings, workshops, conferences, publications. Membership, $295-695.

TRI-COUNTY COMMUNITY ACTION PROGRAM

2410 Oak Street
Brainerd, MN 56401
(218) 829-2410
Fax—(218) 829-0494

P.O. Box 368
Little Falls, MN 56345
(320) 632-3691
Fax—(320) 632-3695

Small business assistance for startup or experienced business owners in Crow Wing, Morrison and Todd Counties who meet income requirements. Offers workshops/seminars on business plans, marketing, record-keeping; counseling for completing loan applications. Call for appointment. Free to eligible individuals.

U.S. SMALL BUSINESS ADMINISTRATION

610-C Butler Square, 100 No. 6th Street
Minneapolis, MN 55403
(612) 370-2324   Fax—(612) 370-2303

Business assistance program. Free Small Business Start-Up Information Kit includes basic steps for starting a small business, helpful phone numbers, sample business plan outline and financial information. Call or write for further information.

WOMENVENTURE

2324 University Ave. W., Suite 200
St. Paul, MN 55114
(612) 646-3808

Business development program for women and men. Help with business plans, cash flow, marketing, loans, record-keeping. Seminars, business plan development, business owner support group and "last resort" small loan fund. Also offers special program for refugees who want to start businesses. Free orientation Thursdays, 6 p.m. Sliding fee.

EDUCATIONAL
CENTERS

Going back to school is a feasible option for some job seekers. If you are currently between jobs or considering a second career, enrolling in a class or full-time educational program can sharpen your job marketability or recharge dated skills. Short-term programs can also provide you with training in backup skills that can help you earn a living during transitional periods in your life.

This section provides brief profiles on the following:

◆ Community and Technical Colleges

◆ Public Colleges and Universities

◆ Private Colleges, Universities and Training Centers

Many schools that cater to adult students offer flexible scheduling to help individuals balance work, family and studies. The newest convenience is the introduction of electronic classrooms, online courses you can access through the Internet from the comfort of your home PC.

A growing number of schools and training centers host Internet sites where you can tap more detailed information about their educational programs. For your convenience, Internet addresses are included in the following listings. **CollegeNET** is an online guide to nationwide educational centers with links to Minnesota colleges on the World Wide Web. CollegeNET Internet address: http://205.199.39.2/

STATE COMMUNITY COLLEGES

State community colleges offer a variety of two-year degree programs to meet occupational and educational objectives. Most provide full- and part-time options. Day, evening, weekend and summer classes are available.

Recently the Minnesota community colleges merged with the state technical college system. This merger has already resulted in a series of administrative and name changes at some institutions. During this period of transition, it is likely that the phone numbers listed below will continue to link you to the information you need.

**ANOKA-RAMSEY
COMMUNITY COLLEGE**
11200 Mississippi Blvd. N.W.
Coon Rapids, MN 55433
(612) 427-2600

AUSTIN COMMUNITY COLLEGE
1600 N.W. 8th Avenue
Austin, MN 55912
(507) 433-0505
(800) 747-6941

CAMBRIDGE COMMUNITY COLLEGE
33270 Polk St. N.E.
Cambridge, MN 55008
(320) 689-7000

**CENTRAL LAKES
COMMUNITY COLLEGE**
501 W. College Drive
Brainerd, MN 56401
(218) 828-2525

**CENTURY COMMUNITY &
TECHNICAL COLLEGE**
3401 Century Ave. No.
White Bear Lake, MN 55110
(612) 779-3200

**FERGUS FALLS
COMMUNITY COLLEGE**
414 College Way
Fergus Falls, MN 56537
(218) 739-7500

**FOND DU LAC
COMMUNITY COLLEGE**
2101 14th Street
Cloquet, MN 55720
(218) 879-0800

HIBBING COMMUNITY COLLEGE
1515 East 25th Street
Hibbing, MN 55746
(218) 262-6700

INVER HILLS COMM. COLLEGE
2500 80th Street East
Inver Grove Heights, MN 55076
(612) 450-8500

ITASCA COMMUNITY COLLEGE
1851 E. Hwy. 169
Grand Rapids, MN 55744
(218) 327-4460

LAKE SUPERIOR COLLEGE
1309 Rice Lake Road
Duluth, MN 55811
(218) 723-4796

MESABI COMMUNITY COLLEGE
1001 W. Chestnut Street
Virginia, MN 55792
(218) 749-7000

MPLS. COMMUNITY COLLEGE
1501 Hennepin Avenue
Minneapolis, MN 55403
(612) 341-7000

NORMANDALE COMM. COLLEGE
9700 France Ave. So.
Bloomington, MN 55431
(612) 832-6320

**NORTH HENNEPIN
COMMUNITY COLLEGE**
7411 85th Ave. No.
Brooklyn Park, MN 55445
(612) 424-0722

**NORTHLAND COMMUNITY &
TECHNICAL COLLEGE**
1101 Highway One East
Thief River Falls, MN 56701
(218) 681-2181   (800) 628-9918

**RAINY-RIVER
COMMUNITY COLLEGE**
1501 Hwy. 71
International Falls, MN 56649
(218) 285-7722   (800) 456-3996

ROCHESTER COMMUNITY COLLEGE
851 30th Ave. S.E.
Rochester, MN 55904
(507) 285-7210

VERMILION COMMUNITY COLLEGE
1900 E. Camp Street
Ely, MN 55731
(218) 365-7207

WILLMAR COMMUNITY COLLEGE
P.O. Box 797, County Rd. 24
Willmar, MN 56201
(320) 231-5102

**WORTHINGTON
COMMUNITY COLLEGE**
1450 College Way
Worthington, MN 56187
(507) 372-2107   (800) 657-3966

STATE TECHNICAL COLLEGES

State-funded two-year technical colleges offer majors in accounting and business, health and personal services, electronics, manufacturing and transportation. Day, evening and weekend classes are offered year-round.

Recently the Minnesota technical college system merged with the state community colleges. This merger has already resulted in a series of administrative and name changes at some institutions. During this period of transition, it is likely that the phone numbers below will continue to link you to the information you need.

ALBERT LEA TECHNICAL COLLEGE
2200 Tech Drive
Albert Lea, MN 56007
(507) 373-0656
(800) 333-2584

ALEXANDRIA TECHNICAL COLLEGE
1601 Jefferson Street
Alexandria, MN 56308
(320) 762-0221
(800) 253-9884

**ANOKA-HENNEPIN
TECHNICAL COLLEGE**
1355 West Highway 10
Anoka, MN 55303
(612) 427-1880

CENTRAL LAKES COLLEGE
300 Quince Street
Brainerd, MN 56401
(218) 828-5344   (800) 247-2574

**CENTURY COMMUNITY
& TECHNICAL COLLEGE**
3300 Century Ave. No.
White Bear Lake, MN 55110
(612) 779-5827

**DAKOTA COUNTY
TECHNICAL COLLEGE**
1300 E. 145th Street
Rosemount, MN 55068
(612) 423-8301

HENNEPIN TECHNICAL COLLEGE
1820 North Xenium Lane
Plymouth, MN 55441-3790
(612) 559-3535

HUTCHINSON TECHNICAL COLLEGE
2 Century Avenue
Hutchinson, MN 55350
(320) 587-3636
(800) 222-4424

LAKE SUPERIOR COLLEGE
2101 Trinity Road
Duluth, MN 55811-3399
(218) 722-2801
(800) 432-2884

MANKATO TECHNICAL COLLEGE
1920 Lee Blvd.
North Mankato, MN 56002
(507) 625-3441
(800) 722-9359

MINNEAPOLIS TECHNICAL COLLEGE
1415 Hennepin Avenue
Minneapolis, MN 55403
(612) 370-9400

MINNESOTA RIVERLAND TECHNICAL COLLEGE
1900 8th Ave. N.W.
Austin, MN 55912
(507) 433-0600
(800) 247-5039

MINNESOTA RIVERLAND TECHNICAL COLLEGE
1225 S.W. Third Street
Faribault, MN 55021
(507) 334-3965
(800) 422-0391

MINNESOTA RIVERLAND TECHNICAL COLLEGE
1926 College View Road S.E.
Rochester, MN 55904
(507) 285-8631
(800) 247-1296

NORTHLAND COMMUNITY & TECHNICAL COLLEGE
1101 Highway One East
Thief River Falls, MN 56701
(218) 681-2181   (800) 628-9918

NORTHWEST TECHNICAL COLLEGE
905 Grant Ave. S.E.
Bemidji, MN 56601
(218) 759-3200   (800) 942-8324

NORTHWEST TECHNICAL COLLEGE
900 Highway 34 East
Detroit Lakes, MN 56501
(218) 847-1341   (800) 492-4836

NORTHWEST TECHNICAL COLLEGE
Highway 220 No.
P.O. Box 111
East Grand Forks, MN 56721
(218) 773-3441
(800) 451-3441

NORTHWEST TECHNICAL COLLEGE
1900 28th Ave. So.
Moorhead, MN 56560
(218) 236-6277   (800) 426-5603

NORTHWEST TECHNICAL COLLEGE
405 Colfax Ave. S.W.
Wadena, MN 56482
(218) 631-3530   (800) 247-2007

PINE TECHNICAL COLLEGE
1000 Fourth Street
Pine City, MN 55063
(320) 629-6764   (800) 521-7463

STATE TECHNICAL COLLEGES cont.

RANGE TECHNICAL COLLEGE
Hwy. 53
P.O. Box 0648
Eveleth, MN 55734
(218) 744-3302   (800) 345-2884

RANGE TECHNICAL COLLEGE
2900 E. Beltline
Hibbing, MN 55746
(218) 262-7200   (800) 433-9989

RED WING TECHNICAL COLLEGE
308 Pioneer Road
Red Wing, MN 55066
(612) 388-8271
(800) 657-4849

ST. CLOUD TECHNICAL COLLEGE
1540 Northway Drive
St. Cloud, MN 56303
(320) 654-5000

ST. PAUL TECHNICAL COLLEGE
235 Marshall Avenue
St. Paul, MN 55102
(612) 221-1300

**SOUTHWESTERN
TECHNICAL COLLEGE**
1011 First St. West
Canby, MN 56220
(507) 223-7252   (800) 658-2535

**SOUTHWESTERN
TECHNICAL COLLEGE**
1593 11th Avenue
Granite Falls, MN 56241
(320) 564-4511   (800) 657-3247

**SOUTHWESTERN
TECHNICAL COLLEGE**
401 West Street
Jackson, MN 56143
(507) 847-3320   (800) 658-2522

**SOUTHWESTERN
TECHNICAL COLLEGE**
1314 No. Hiawatha Avenue
P.O. Box 250
Pipestone, MN 56164
(507) 825-5471   (800) 658-2330

WILLMAR TECHNICAL COLLEGE
2101 15th Ave. N.W.
P.O. Box 1097
Willmar, MN 56201
(320) 235-5114   (800) 722-1151

WINONA TECHNICAL COLLEGE
1250 Homer Road
Winona, MN 55987
(507) 454-4600   (800) 372-8164

COLLEGES, UNIVERSITIES & TRAINING CENTERS

ACADEMY EDUCATION CENTER

3050 Metro Drive, Suite 200
Minneapolis, MN 55425
(612) 851-0066   Fax—(612) 851-0094

Certificate and degree programs in accounting, aviation and computers.

AUGSBURG COLLEGE

2211 Riverside Avenue
Minneapolis, MN 55454
(612) 330-1001   (800) 788-5678   Fax—(612) 330-1590
Internet address: http://www.augsburg.edu

Four-year private liberal arts college. Day and weekend programs.

BROWN INSTITUTE

2225 E. Lake Street
Minneapolis, MN 55407
(612) 721-2481   (800) 627-6966   Fax—(612) 721-2179
E-mail: browni@winternet.com

Two-year art, business, broadcasting and technical college. Day and
evening classes, year-round.

COLLEGE OF VISUAL ARTS
(Formerly College of Associated Arts)

344 Summit Avenue
St. Paul, MN 55102
(612) 224-3416   Fax—(612) 224-8854

Four-year private visual arts college. Degrees in communication design,
photography, illustration, painting, drawing, printmaking and sculpture.
Full- and part-time day program.

COLLEGE OF ST. CATHERINE

Minneapolis Campus	St. Paul Campus
601 25th Avenue So.	2004 Randolph Avenue
Minneapolis, MN 55454	St. Paul, MN 55105
(612) 690-7700	(612) 690-6505 (800) 945-4599
Fax—(612) 690-7849	Fax—(612) 690-6024

Internet address: http://www.stkate.edu

Academic school. Four-year private liberal arts college for women. Day, evening, weekend and summer classes. Graduate and online courses.

CONCORDIA COLLEGE

275 North Syndicate Street
St. Paul, MN 55104
(612) 641-8230   (800) 333-4705   Fax—(612) 659-0207
E-mail: admiss@luther.csp.edu

Four-year private liberal arts college. Full- and part-time schedules.

DUNWOODY INSTITUTE

818 Dunwoody Blvd.
Minneapolis, MN 55403-1192
(612) 374-5800   (800) 292-4625   Fax—(612) 374-4128
E-mail: @dunwoody.tec.mn.us

Technical vocational school. Two-year or short-term programs in automotive, drafting, baking, electrical, refrigeration, printing, machine tool technology. Full- and part-time programs, days and evenings.

ELECTRONIC UNIVERSITY NETWORK

1977 Colestin Road
Hornbrook, CA 96044
(541) 482-5871   Fax—(541) 482-7544
E-mail: eunhello@aol.com

University degrees earned online through America Online.

HAMLINE UNIVERSITY
1536 Hewitt Avenue
St. Paul, MN 55104
(612) 641-2800   Fax—(612) 641-2030
Internet address: http://www.hamline.edu/

Private liberal arts university and Minnesota's first university. Call for full-time and other program information.

LOWTHIAN COLLEGE
825 Second Ave. So.
Minneapolis, MN 55402
(612) 332-3361   (800) 777-3643

Private college. Associate degrees in retail merchandising management, interior/fashion design. Full- and part-time programs, days, evenings and weekends.

MACALESTER COLLEGE
1600 Grand Avenue
St. Paul, MN 55105
(612) 696-6357   (800) 231-7974   Fax—(612) 696-6724
Internet address: gopher://gopher.macalstr.edu/

Four-year private liberal arts college. Full- and part-time day programs.

METROPOLITAN STATE UNIVERSITY
Minneapolis Campus
710 Hennepin Avenue
Minneapolis, MN 55403
(612) 341-7250

St. Paul Campus
700 E. Seventh Street
St. Paul, MN 55106
(612) 772-7600

Internet address: http://www.metro.msus.edu/
E-mail: nancy_driessen@metro2.metro.msus.edu

Four-year state university. Variety of majors or individualized program to design a degree. Day, evening, weekend classes, year-round.

TWIN CITIES

MINNEAPOLIS BUSINESS COLLEGE

1711 W. County Road B
Roseville, MN 55113
(612) 636-7406   (800) 279-5200   Fax—(612) 636-8185

Programs for travel/hospitality, accounting, graphic design, legal secretarial, office administration, computer programming and medical assistants. Fourteen month degree, eight month diploma programs. Day classes only.

MINNEAPOLIS COLLEGE OF ART AND DESIGN

2501 Stevens Ave. So.
Minneapolis, MN 55404
(612) 874-3760   (800) 874-6223   Fax—(612) 874-3711
Internet address: http://www.mcad.edu/

Private professional college of visual arts. Offers day and evening classes, year-round. BFA, MFA degrees.

MINNEAPOLIS DRAFTING SCHOOL

5700 West Broadway
Minneapolis, MN 55428
(612) 535-8843   (800) 878-3729
Fax—(612) 535-9205

Private post-secondary technical school. Major programs in architectural or engineering design/drafting. Special programs for college graduates.

MINNESOTA SCHOOL OF REAL ESTATE INC.

7148 Shady Oak Road
Eden Prairie, MN 55344
(612) 829-0101   (800) 737-6776
Fax—(612) 829-0801

Continuing education for real estate appraisers, insurance, building contractors, attorneys and assessors. Day and weekend classes.

NATIONAL COLLEGE

1380 Energy Lane, Suite 13
St. Paul, MN 55108
(612) 644-1265   Fax—(612) 644-0690

Private college. Bachelor and associate degrees, diploma programs in business administration, computer information systems, travel and tourism, applied management. Full/part-time, days, evenings, weekends.

NORTHWEST TECHNICAL INSTITUTE

11995 Singletree Lane
Eden Prairie, MN 55344
(612) 944-0080   Fax—(612) 944-9274

Two-year private technical institute. Programs in engineering or architectural drafting/design and CAD technology.

RASMUSSEN COLLEGE

12450 Wayzata Blvd., Suite 315
Minnetonka, MN 55305
(612) 545-2000   (800) 852-0929
Fax—(612) 545-7038

Short-term degree/diploma programs in court reporting, travel, medical records, medical/legal secretary, business, office and management careers. Day and evening classes. Two metro campuses.

SCHOOL OF COMMUNICATION ARTS

2526 27th Ave. So.
Minneapolis, MN 55406
(612) 721-5357   (800) 800-2835
Fax—(612) 721-6642
E-mail: sca3d@aol.com

Private college with majors in advanced computer animation and computer graphics, video, photography and multimedia.

UNIVERSITY OF MINNESOTA
Twin Cities Campus

240 Williamson Hall
231 Pillsbury Drive S.E.
Minneapolis, MN 55455
(612) 625-2008
(612) 625-0000 VISITLINE for tours and campus visits
(800) 752-1000   TTY—(612) 625-9051
Fax—(612) 626-1693
Internet address: http://www.umn.edu/

Four-year public university. Undergraduate, graduate and professional programs. Continuing education and extension divisions. Day, evening and summer classes.

UNIVERSITY OF ST. THOMAS

2115 Summit Avenue
St. Paul, MN 55105
(612) 962-6150   (800) 328-6819   Fax—(612) 962-6160
Internet address: http://www.stthomas.edu/

Four-year private liberal arts college. Classes offered year-round. New College offers weekend and evening courses.

UNIVERSITY ONLINE

12372 River Ridge Blvd.
Burnsville, MN 55337
(612) 882-8859   Fax—(612) 882-9771
Internet address: http://www.uol.com
E-mail: info@uol.com

Offers online academic, technical and business courses from grade school through college levels. Duration of classes depends on individual schedules. Requires computer and access to the Internet.

GREATER MINNESOTA

ARROWHEAD UNIVERSITY CENTER

1515 E. 25th Street
Hibbing, MN 55746
(218) 262-6753   (800) 369-4970   Fax—(218) 262-6791

Upper division and master degree credits can be earned through extension classes held at community college campuses in northeastern Minnesota.

BEMIDJI STATE UNIVERSITY

1500 Birchmont Drive N.E.
Bemidji, MN 56601-2699
(218) 755-2000   (800) 475-2001   Fax—(218) 755-4048
Internet address: http://www.bemidji.msus.edu/

Four-year public university offering degrees in liberal arts. Full- and part-time weekday and summer classes.

CARLETON COLLEGE

100 South College
Northfield, MN 55057
(507) 663-4190   (800) 995-2275
Fax—(507) 933-4526
Internet address: http://www.carleton.edu/

Four-year private liberal arts college. Full-time weekday classes.

COLLEGE OF ST. BENEDICT

37 So. College Avenue
St. Joseph, MN 56374
(320) 363-5308   (800) 544-1489
Fax—(320) 363-5010
Internet address: http://www.CSBSJU.edu/index.html

Private liberal arts college for women. Offers more than 40 majors and pre-professional programs in partnership with St. John's University.

COLLEGE OF ST. SCHOLASTICA

1200 Kenwood Avenue
Duluth, MN 55811
(218) 723-6046   (800) 447-5444   Fax—(218) 723-6290
Internet address: http://www.css.edu/
Private liberal arts college. Full-time, part-time and summer classes.

CONCORDIA COLLEGE

901 So. 8th Street
Moorhead, MN 56562
(218) 299-3004   (800) 699-9897   Fax—(218) 299-3947
Internet address: http://www.cord.edu/
Four-year private liberal arts college. Classes full- and part-time.

DULUTH BUSINESS UNIVERSITY

412 W. Superior Street
Duluth, MN 55802
(218) 722-3361   (800) 777-8406   Fax—(218) 722-8376
Private academic college. Flexible day/evening schedules.

GUSTAVUS ADOLPHUS COLLEGE

800 W. College Avenue
St. Peter, MN 56082
(507) 933-7676   (800) 487-8288   Fax—(507) 933-6270
Internet address: http://www.gac.edu/
Four-year private liberal arts college. Full-time weekday classes.

MANKATO STATE UNIVERSITY

P.O. Box 8400, Mankato, MN 56002
(507) 389-1822   (800) 722-0544
Internet address: http://www.mankato.msus.edu/
Four-year public liberal arts university. Full- and part-time, year-round.

GREATER MINNESOTA

MOORHEAD STATE UNIVERSITY
1104 7th Avenue So.
Moorhead, MN 56563
(218) 236-2011   (800) 593-7246   Fax—(218) 236-2885
Internet address: http://www.moorhead.msus.edu
Four-year public university offers degrees in the liberal arts. Flexible schedules.

RASMUSSEN BUSINESS COLLEGE
245 37th Avenue No.
St. Cloud, MN 56303
(320) 251-5600
(800) 852-0460
Fax—(320) 251-3702

501 Holly Lane
Mankato, MN 56001
(507) 625-6556
(800) 657-6767
Fax—(507) 625-6557

Two-year private business and vocational school. Training in computerized accounting, secretarial, court reporting, sales, travel-business, accounting, word processing programs. Weekday, evening and summer classes.

ST. CLOUD HOSPITAL HEALTH CARE SCHOOLS
1406 Sixth Avenue No.
St. Cloud, MN 56303
(320) 255-5632—School of Medical Technology
(320) 255-5719—School of X-Ray Technology
Health care technology training school.

ST. CLOUD STATE UNIVERSITY
720 Fourth Avenue So.
St. Cloud, MN 56301
(320) 255-2244   (800) 369-4260   Fax—(320) 654-5367
Internet address: http://www.stcloud.msus.edu/
Public university. Undergraduate and graduate programs in business, education, fine arts, humanities, science, technology and social sciences.

GREATER MINNESOTA

ST. JOHN'S UNIVERSITY

Collegeville, MN 56321

(320) 363-2196   (800) 245-6467

Fax—(320) 363-3206

Internet address: http://www.csbsju.edu/

Private liberal arts college for men. Graduate school of theology for men and women.

SAINT MARY'S UNIVERSITY OF MINNESOTA

700 Terrace Heights, Campus Box #2

Winona, MN 55987

(507) 457-1700   (800) 635-5987

Fax—(507) 457-1633

Internet address: http://140.190.128.190/SMC/HomePage.html

Four-year private liberal arts college. Full-time and part-time, weekday classes.

ST. OLAF COLLEGE

1520 St. Olaf Avenue

Northfield, MN 55057-1098

(507) 646-3025   (800) 800-3025

Fax—(507) 646-3832

Internet address: http://www.stolaf.edu/

Four-year private liberal arts college. Full- and part-time programs. Weekday and summer classes.

SOUTHWEST STATE UNIVERSITY

1501 State Street

Marshall, MN 56258

(507) 537-6286   (800) 642-0684

Fax—(507) 537-7154

Four-year public liberal arts university. Full/part-time programs.

GREATER MINNESOTA

UNIVERSITY OF MINNESOTA
Crookston Campus
Hwy. 2 and 75 North
Crookston, MN 56716
(218) 281-6510   (800) 232-6466   Fax—(218) 281-8050
Internet address: http://www.crk.umn.edu
Four-year public college. Day and evening classes offered year-round.

UNIVERSITY OF MINNESOTA
Duluth Campus
10 University Drive
Duluth, MN 55812
(218) 726-7171   (800) 232-1339   Fax—(218) 726-6144
Four-year public university. Undergraduate, graduate and professional programs. Day, evening, summer classes.

UNIVERSITY OF MINNESOTA
Morris Campus
105 Behmler Hall
Morris, MN 56267
(320) 589-6035   (800) 992-8863   Fax—(320) 589-1673
Four-year public university offering degrees in liberal arts. Full-time, part-time and evening programs.

WINONA STATE UNIVERSITY
P.O. Box 5838
Winona, MN 55987
(507) 457-5000   (800) 242-8978   Fax—(507) 457-5620
Internet address: http://www.winona.msus.edu/
Four-year public liberal arts university. Full and part-time.

RETIREMENT

PLANNING

Ever since you filled out your first job application, you've probably fantasized about retirement. Who doesn't dream about trading in rush hour commutes for a second cup of morning coffee? Or exchanging deadlines and daily planners for long, lazy summers at the cabin?

If you're age 50 or 60-something and recently out of a job, early retirement may be an enticing option. Even if you are currently employed but your employer has presented a tempting early retirement package, the offer may seem too good to refuse.

But here's the catch: Retirement planning is serious business. Experts say that, without good planning, you could face many future years with a short-fall of income.

◆ Look before you leap. Ask serious questions and get expert advice. There are many types of professionals to turn to for answers: financial planners, tax accountants and attorneys, to name a few. Many local community education departments also offer classes on retirement planning.

◆ With limited space, we couldn't list all of the retirement planning experts in Minnesota. Instead we've opted to include these non-profit resources that offer free or low-cost services to help you make savvy retirement decisions.

AARP
American Association of Retired Persons
Publications Fulfillment, 601 E Street N.W.
Washington, DC 20077-1214
(202) 434-2277

AARP is the nation's largest organization of people, age 50 and older. Publications addressing retirement planning and job-seeking materials include: "Look Before You Leap: A Guide to Early Retirement Incentive Programs," "How to Stay Employable for Mid-Life and Older Workers," "Single Person's Guide to Retirement Planning," "Working Options: How to Plan Your Job Search and Work Life" and more. Call or write for publications directory. Single copies are free.

CENTER FOR CAREER CHANGE
Minnesota Senior Federation
1885 University Ave. W., Suite 190
St. Paul, MN 55104
(612) 645-0261   (800) 365-8765   Fax—(612) 641-8969

Open to the public. Offers full range of retirement planning and counseling services. Provides individualized assistance with pension and retirement issues including legal and technical assistance. Call for information. Fees: $35 per session.

CENTER FOR SENIOR CITIZEN'S EDUCATION
University of St. Thomas
2115 Summit Avenue, LOR 309
St. Paul, MN 55105
(612) 962-5188

Open to the public and targeted to individuals, ages 55 and older. Services include individualized retirement counseling and financial planning provided by professionals with expertise in law, insurance, finance, etc. Also offers university classes at no charge to qualified participants. Call for information. Services are free.

5

FOR NETWORKING & SUPPORT

◆ Job Support Groups

◆ Networking Groups

◆ Crisis & Referral Helplines

◆ Health & Money Interim Options

◆ Relocation Resources

J ob hunting is a social process. And this chapter is your "people" connection. Don't go through your job hunt alone. There are more resources than you think to help you stay afloat and connected to the community during this transition.

Job support groups and networking organizations are prime places to expand your contacts, learn new skills and feel good about who you are and what you have to offer.

If you are experiencing personal or household difficulties, there are services to reach out and give you a hand. Crisis and referral helplines offer immediate leads to community support services. Other transition services can help you sort out concerns about healthcare or personal finances so you can take positive steps to put your life in order.

Relocation resources can give you a foothold in a new community if a work opportunity requires a long-distance move.

JOB SUPPORT

GROUPS

Here's a bit of advice we hope you'll take:

Get thee to a job support group.

Job support groups can provide greatly needed emotional support to job seekers. They also can offer practical no-cost job-search information provided by career experts invited as guest speakers.

Most job support groups are free and open to the public, held at local churches and synagogues on a drop-in basis. At regular meetings, job seekers gather to support each other through the transition process. Participants share job-search strategies and weekly progress reports. They also support each other in dealing with the emotional and financial challenges connected with losing a job.

Twin Cities groups usually attract 10-35 people per meeting. Some groups also invite spouses and partners. Though reservations are rarely required, it's a good idea to contact the sponsoring organization prior to attending to confirm the meeting schedule.

If your community would like to start a job support group, **Jobs in Transition 'N Support Group, Inc.,** a non-profit corporation, assists in establishing new job support groups statewide. Call or write for information: Jobs in Transition 'N Support Group, Inc., 2150 Third Street, White Bear Lake, MN 55110. Telephone, (612) 429-9594.

BASILICA OF ST. MARY
Job Transition Support Group
88 North 17th Street
Minneapolis, MN 55403
(612) 333-1381   Fax—(612) 333-7230

Open to the public. The support group meets on the third Thursday of each month from 7-8:30 p.m. and provides sharing, support, education, information and occasional speakers. Call for information. No charge.

CENACLE RETREAT HOUSE
Retreat for the Unemployed
1221 Wayzata Blvd.
Wayzata, MN 55391
(612) 473-7308   Fax—(612) 473-8571

January weekend retreat for unemployed and spouses. Focuses on faith, courage and morale. Open to public. Call for reservations. No charge.

CENTENNIAL UNITED METHODIST CHURCH
Job Transition Support Group
1524 West County Road C-2
Roseville, MN 55113
(612) 633-7644

Open to the public. Offers on-going support and job seeking assistance to participants. Call for information and schedule. No charge.

CENTRAL LUTHERAN CHURCH
Jobs in Transition 'N Support Group
1103 School Street
Elk River, MN 55330
(612) 441-2363   Fax—(612) 441-0010

Open to the public. Speakers, group discussions, emotional support, networking opportunities. Call for information and schedule. No charge.

CHRIST PRESBYTERIAN CHURCH
Job Transition Support Group

6901 Normandale Road
Edina, MN 55435
(612) 920-8515   Fax—(612) 920-4775

Meets alternate Saturdays, 8:30 a.m. Focuses on emotional and spiritual needs of participants. Discussions and presentations on job-search strategies, emotional conflicts, stages of grief due to job loss. Drop in. No charge.

CHRIST THE KING CHURCH

1900 7th St. N.W.
New Brighton, MN 55112
(612) 633-4674

Meets monthly, first and third Tuesdays. Church provides job-search resource notebook on loan to interested individuals. Call for information. No charge.

COLONIAL CHURCH OF EDINA
Job Transition Support Group

6200 Colonial Way
Edina, MN 55436
(612) 925-2711   Fax—(612) 925-1591

Open to the public. Meets Mondays at 7 p.m. Generally attracts 30-50 participants. Speakers on first and third Mondays on topics like personal marketing, employment alternatives, coping with job loss. On alternate Mondays, informal networking and small groups. Drop in. No charge.

EAST SIDE NEIGHBORHOOD SERVICE, INC.

1929 Second St. N.E.
Minneapolis, MN 55418
(612) 781-6011

Open to the public. Series of job-search workshops with speakers and small group discussion. Access to computer database of job listings. Call for information. No charge.

FIRST EVANGELICAL LUTHERAN CHURCH
Jobs in Transition 'N Support Group

4000 Linden Street
White Bear Lake, MN 55110
(612) 429-9594   Fax—(612) 426-0466

Meets Mondays, 7-9 p.m. Weekly meetings with informational speakers, small-group discussions, networking opportunities. Database of participants and employers. Access to typewriters and computers. Drop in. No charge.

GRACE LUTHERAN CHURCH
Jobs in Transition 'N Support Group

13655 Round Lake Blvd.
Andover, MN 55304
(612) 421-6520

Meets Wednesdays, 7-9 p.m. Guest speakers on alternate weeks. Topics covered include networking, computers, resume writing and other areas of interest to job seekers. Call to confirm schedule. Drop in. No charge.

HENNEPIN AVENUE UNITED METHODIST CHURCH
Hennepin Job Transition

Lyndale and Groveland
Minneapolis, MN 55403
(612) 871-5303   Fax—(612) 871-4684

Meets first and third Tuesdays, 7-9 p.m. Information on job seeking and transition, and resource materials. Call for information. No charge.

MINNEAPOLIS JOB SUPPORT WORKSHOP

3033 Excelsior Blvd., Suite 300
Minneapolis, MN 55416
Phone/Fax—(612) 929-2225

Meets Wednesdays, 7 p.m. Programs on interviewing, resumes, networking, phone calling, problem solving. Drop in. No charge.

PAX CHRISTI CATHOLIC COMMUNITY
In Transition

12100 Pioneer Trail
Eden Prairie, MN 55347
(612) 941-3150

Open to job seekers, spouses and partners. Meets first and third Sundays, 7-8:30 p.m. Offers discussion, support, job-search direction, networking opportunities. Guest speakers at each meeting. Drop in. No charge.

PILLSBURY NEIGHBORHOOD SERVICES, INC.
Job Seeker's Support Group

Coyle Center, 420 15th Ave. So.
Minneapolis, MN 55454
(612) 338-5282

Open to Minneapolis residents. Informal discussions about unemployment and job-search issues. Call for information. No charge.

ST. ALPHONSUS CHURCH JOB CLUB

CCD Building
4111 71st Ave. No.
Brooklyn Center, MN 55429
(612) 561-5100

Open to the public. Meets Mondays, 9 a.m. Group provides mutual support, information, strategies and job leads. Drop in. No charge.

ST. ANDREW LUTHERAN CHURCH
Job Transition Group

13600 Technology Drive
Eden Prairie, MN 55344
(612) 937-2776

Open to the public. Job support group meets Wednesdays at 11:30 a.m. Participants provide support, networking tips and share updates about their personal job search. No charge.

TWIN CITIES

ST. EDWARDS CATHOLIC CHURCH
Job Transition Group
9401 Nesbitt Ave. So.
Bloomington, MN 55437
(612) 835-7101

Meets second and fourth Tuesdays, 7:30-9 p.m. Informal meetings provide support, networking, occasional speakers. Drop in or call. No charge.

TAPS' JOB CLUB
Epilepsy Foundations of Minnesota and America
777 Raymond Ave.
St. Paul, MN 55114
(612) 646-8675   (800) 779-0777

TAPS (Training Applicants for Placement Success) is targeted to people with epilepsy. Meets Tuesdays, 10-11:30 a.m. Guest speakers, group discussion, peer counseling on employment issues. Call for information and to schedule an appointment prior to attending. No charge.

TWIN CITIES MEN'S CENTER (TMC)
3249 Hennepin Ave. So., Suite 55
Minneapolis, MN 55408
(612) 822-5892

Support groups focusing on transition issues. Open to men; some to men and women. Call for St. Paul location. Free or voluntary donation.

WOMENVENTURE
Job Search Support Group for Women
2324 University Ave. W., Suite 200
St. Paul, MN 55114
(612) 646-3808

Open to the public. Meets Tuesdays, 10-11:30 a.m., and Wednesday evenings, 6-7:30 p.m. Facilitated group for women offers on-going encouragement during the job search. Drop in. No charge.

NETWORKING

GROUPS

Call it Who You Know.
Call it Clout.
Call it Contacts.
Your personal network of
old friends, new friends, acquaintances, co-workers and relatives can help
you get hired.

Networking is the art of expanding your contacts to eventually
reach a potential employer. Case in point: Seventy percent of all
job seekers directly contact employers to inquire about unadvertised
positions. How do they know about these jobs?

Networking. And it works.

◆ Business, civic, professional and trade organizations are also
useful for expanding your network. Become a visible participant at the
associations that serve your profession or industry, and at community,
church, volunteer and civic organizations.

◆ The Internet is a fascinating and convenient way to network
online with peers in your field and other job seekers. See listings for
Internet Employment Resources beginning on page 98.

◆ To track down additional networking organizations, check your
local library for the **Directory of Minnesota Business and Professional
Associations,** published by the James J. Hill Reference Library, 80 W.
Fourth St., St. Paul, MN 55102, (612) 227-9531. This directory identifies
about 300 Minnesota trade associations and professional societies.

ADVERTISING FEDERATION OF MINNESOTA

430 First Ave. No., Suite 401
Minneapolis, MN 55401
(612) 339-5470   Fax—(612) 339-5818

Serving individuals in advertising. Offers continuing education, monthly professional development seminars, networking opportunities. Call for information. Annual dues, $130.

AIA MINNESOTA

275 Market St., Suite 54
Minneapolis, MN 55405
(612) 338-6763   Fax—(612) 338-7981

Professional association for architects. Offers job bank of current job openings and resume referral service. Membership not required.

AMERICAN INSTITUTE OF GRAPHIC ARTS
Minnesota Chapter

275 Market St., Suite 54
Minneapolis, MN 55405
(612) 339-6904   Fax—(612) 338-7981

Serving individuals in graphic arts. Offers networking opportunities, job book, resume book and positions available ads in monthly newsletter. Call or write for information and annual membership dues. Sliding fee.

AMERICAN MARKETING ASSOCIATION
Minnesota Chapter

4248 Park Glen Road
Minneapolis, MN 55416
(612) 927-4262   Fax—(612) 929-1318

Serving professionals in marketing, market research and sales. Provides educational and networking services. Distributes listings of job openings to members. National organization also publishes job vacancies.

AMERICAN SOCIETY OF MECHANICAL ENGINEERS
555 Park St.
St. Paul, MN 55103
(612) 942-1340—Minnesota Chapter   (800) 628-6437—Membership
Serving mechanical engineers. Regional/national job bulletin, computer job bank, reduced meeting fees and dues abatement for unemployed, job fairs, free resume database, on-line service to investigate career opportunities.

AMERICAN SOCIETY OF WOMEN ACCOUNTANTS
Minneapolis/St. Paul Chapter
10488 Washington Blvd. N.E.
Blaine, MN 55434
(612) 755-1608
Professional association for women accountants. Membership publications include job listings and positions wanted ads.

APICS—TWIN CITIES
Educational Society for Resource Management
10313 Virginia Road
Bloomington, MN 55438
(612) 941-7305   Fax—(612) 941-8668
Serving individuals in materials/operations management. Offers resume file service. Job vacancies are announced at meetings. Call for information. Annual dues, $110.

CARE PROVIDERS OF MINNESOTA
2850 Metro Dr., Suite 200
Bloomington, MN 55425
(612) 854-2844   Fax—(612) 854-6214
Serving long-term care and senior housing providers. Offers resume database, networking opportunities, positions wanted/available ads for administrators in member publications. Reduced fees on publications for unemployed. Call for information and dues.

CHAMBERS OF COMMERCE

Many Chambers of Commerce publish lists identifying local networking organizations. Below is a sampling of Minnesota Chambers. Refer to your area phone directory for other Chamber offices.

BEMIDJI CHAMBER
300 Bemidji Ave.
Bemidji, MN 56619-0850
(218) 751-3541   (800) 458-2223
Free list of organizations.

DULUTH CHAMBER
118 E. Superior Street
Duluth, MN 55802
(218) 722-5501
Free list of organizations.

FARIBAULT CHAMBER
530 Wilson Ave.
Faribault, MN 55021
(507) 334-4381   (800) 658-2354
Organizations list, $25.

GRAND RAPIDS CHAMBER
One N.W. Third Street
Grand Rapids, MN 55744
(218) 326-6619   (800) 472-6366
Free list of organizations.

HIBBING CHAMBER
211 E. Howard Street
Hibbing, MN 55746
(218) 262-3895   (800) 444-2246
Fax—(218) 262-3897
Free list of organizations.

MANKATO CHAMBER
112 Riverfront Drive
Mankato, MN 56001
(507) 345-4519   (800) 657-4733
Free list of organizations.

MOORHEAD CHAMBER
725 Center Avenue
Moorhead, MN 56560
(218) 236-6200
Organizations list, $5.

OWATONNA CHAMBER
320 Hoffman Drive
Owatonna, MN 55060
(507) 451-7970   (800) 423-6466
Organizations list, $10.

ROCHESTER CHAMBER
220 S. Broadway, Suite 100
Rochester, MN 55904
(507) 288-1122
Organizations list, $15.

ST. CLOUD CHAMBER
30 Sixth Ave. South
St. Cloud, MN 56302
(320) 251-2940
Organizations list, $2.

HRP OF MINNESOTA

1711 W. County Road B, Suite 300-N
Roseville, MN 55113
(612) 635-0306   Fax—(612) 635-0307

Serving human resource professionals. Offers networking opportunities, continuing education, positions available/wanted ads in member publications. Annual dues, $40.

INTERNATIONAL ASSOC. OF BUSINESS COMMUNICATORS

P.O. Box 16247
St. Louis Park, MN 55416-0247
(612) 333-4222
Fax—(612) 928-7094

Serving business communications and public relations. Offers job bank, resume referral service, job matching, continuing education and networking opportunities. Call or write for information and dues.

MEETING PROFESSIONALS INTERNATIONAL

Minnesota Chapter

(612) 470-7838

Serving meeting planners, hospitality industry, caterers and suppliers. National association provides access to career counselors at annual conference, industry salary surveys. Annual dues, $260.

MIDWEST DIRECT MARKETING ASSOCIATION

4248 Park Glen Road
Minneapolis, MN 55416
(612) 927-9220
Fax—(612) 929-1318

Serving direct marketing professionals. Member services include resume referral service, networking opportunities. Job vacancies published in member publications. Annual dues, $75.

MINNESOTA BROADCASTERS ASSOCIATION

3517 Raleigh Ave. So., P.O. Box 16030
St. Louis Park, MN 55416
(612) 926-8123   (800) 245-5838   Fax—(612) 926-9761

Serving members of broadcasting industry. Offers resume database, positions wanted ads in monthly newsletter. Membership not required for services.

MINNESOTA BUSINESS BREAKFASTS

Meeting Location:

Edinborough Park, 7700 York Avenue So.
Edina, MN 55435
Reservations: (612) 682-1931   Fax—(612) 682-2043

Networking opportunity open to the public. Generally meets monthly on second and fourth Tuesdays, 7:15-9 a.m. at Edinborough Park. Programs focus on sales and marketing skills, ideas to help non-sales personnel sharpen job-search strategies. Networking encouraged. Call for dates and topics. Tickets, $15 at door, $12 in advance.

MINNESOTA OCCUPATIONAL THERAPY ASSOCIATION

P.O. Box 26532
Minneapolis, MN 55426
(612) 920-0484   Fax—(612) 920-6098

Serving practitioners of occupational therapy. Placement service includes bi-weekly announcements of job vacancies at nominal charge to members only. Call for information.

MINNESOTA RECREATION & PARK ASSOCIATION

5005 West 36th Street
St. Louis Park, MN 55416
(612) 920-6906   (800) 862-3659   Fax—(612) 920-6766

Serving recreation, park and community education professionals. Publishes monthly jobs bulletin identifying 25-100 openings nationwide. Free to members; non-member subscription, $25/year.

MINNESOTA SOCIETY OF CERTIFIED PUBLIC ACCOUNTANTS

7900 Xerxes Ave. So., Suite 1230
Bloomington, MN 55431
(612) 831-2707

Serving certified public accountants. Job matching service to members only.

MINNESOTA SOCIETY OF PROFESSIONAL ENGINEERS

555 Park St., Suite 130
St. Paul, MN 55103
(612) 292-8860   Fax—(612) 292-8737

Serving licensed professional engineers in all disciplines. Monthly membership magazine includes 10-12 job listings per issue.

MINNESOTA SPEECH-LANGUAGE-HEARING ASSOCIATION

P.O. Box 26115, Minneapolis, MN 55426
(612) 920-0787   Fax—(612) 920-6098

Serving speech-language pathology and audiology professions. Networking opportunities, placement service, job ads in member publications.

MINNESOTA TELECOMMUNICATIONS ASSOCIATION

9851 Crestwood Terrace
Minneapolis, MN 55347
(612) 934-8499—General   (612) 591-2173—Job Hotline

Serving telecommunications industry. Networking opportunities, job hotline, continuing education open to members and non-members.

MINNESOTA WOMEN IN THE TRADES

550 Rice Street
St. Paul, MN 55103
(612) 228-9955—General   (612) 228-1271—Job Hotline

Serving women in non-traditional employment. Job hotline, job referral service, networking opportunities. Call for schedule. Annual dues, $25.

NATIONAL ASSOCIATION OF SOCIAL WORKERS

480 Concordia Avenue
St. Paul, MN 55103
(612) 293-1935   Fax—(612) 293-0952

Job opportunities bulletin for members only. Call for information.

NETWORK USA — DOWNTOWN MINNEAPOLIS

601 Second Ave. So., Suite 4400
Minneapolis, MN 55402
(612) 349-7971   Fax—(612) 349-7909

Networking opportunity at Minneapolis Athletic Club. Call for information.

PRINTING INDUSTRY OF MINNESOTA INC.

450 North Syndicate, Suite 200
St. Paul, MN 55104
(612) 646-4826   (800) 448-7566   Fax—(612) 646-8673

Serving Minnesota printing and graphic arts industry. Career materials, resume referral service. Membership not required for these services.

PUBLIC RELATIONS SOCIETY OF AMERICA
Minnesota Chapter

P.O. Box 16247, St. Louis Park, MN 55416-0247
(612) 928-7772   Fax—(612) 928-7094

Serving public relations practitioners. Offers resume referral service to members, free for limited time. Non-members, $25.

SALES AND MARKETING EXECUTIVES

8030 Old Cedar Avenue So., Suite 225
Minneapolis, MN 55425
(612) 854-0109   Fax—(612) 854-1402

Serving executive level sales and marketing management. Networking meetings, job bank, positions ads in member publications.

SOCIETY FOR TECHNICAL COMMUNICATIONS

Twin Cities Chapter

(612) 942-1600

Internet address: http://www.primenet.com/~wai/stc_tc.html

Serving technical communicators. Offers job bank, employment referral service, networking opportunities. Job vacancies announced at meetings. Annual dues, $95.

ST. PAUL LEGAL EMPLOYEES EDUCATIONAL ASSOCIATION

1113 Transit Avenue

Roseville, MN 55113

(612) 347-0629   Fax—(612) 347-0600

Serving legal support staff. Offers positions available ads in member publications, continuing education, networking opportunities, monthly educational speakers and annual spring seminar. Call or write for information. Dues, $10.

THE MANUFACTURERS ALLIANCE

6009 Gettysburg Avenue No.

New Hope, MN 55428

(612) 533-8239   Fax—(612) 535-2326

Serving manufacturers. Offers job bank, resume referral service, continuing education, networking opportunities. Connects employers with job applicants. Call for information and fees.

TWIN CITIES PERSONNEL ASSOCIATION

7630 W. 145th St., Suite 202

Apple Valley, MN 55124

(612) 432-7755—General   (612) 832-3898—Job Hotline

Serving human resource professionals. Networking meetings open to members and non-members. Offers continuing education, job hotline. Annual dues, $50.

TWIN CITIES PROFESSIONAL PART-TIME ASSOCIATION

P.O. Box 1114
Watertown, MN 55388
(612) 897-0302

Provides networking opportunities every other month. Call for information. First guest meeting is free; thereafter, $8. Annual dues, $30.

TWIN CITIES QUALITY ASSURANCE ASSOCIATION

P.O. Box 2799 Loop Station
Minneapolis, MN 55402
(612) 440-6300   Fax—(612) 440-5700

Serving software quality assurance professionals. Provides resume referral service, networking opportunities. Job vacancies announced at monthly meetings. Annual dues, $35.

WOMEN IN COMMUNICATIONS, INC.
Twin Cities Chapter

6145 Club Valley Road
Shorewood, MN 55331
(612) 323-3393   Fax—(612) 474-3949

Serving professional women in communications. Offers resume referral service, free to members; $25, non-members. Resume critique service, $10. Monthly networking meetings, annual career seminar for college students and career changers. Write or call for information.

CRISIS & REFERRAL
HELPLINES

Losing a job puts many folks on an emotional roller coaster. It's not uncommon to feel shocked. Angry. Isolated. Hurt. Depressed. Sad. Or a gamut of other emotions.

Sometimes stress contributes to marital tensions or chemical dependency. Perhaps you require immediate assistance with food, housing, legal concerns, childcare or other basic needs.

Luckily, there is no shortage of help in Minnesota. In this section we've listed helplines that offer:

◆ Information & Referrals

◆ Crisis Counseling

◆ Chemical Dependency

◆ Food, Housing and Childcare

◆ Legal Concerns

For those in crisis now: Many helplines can refer you to community-based support services for immediate assistance. Others provide 24-hour crisis counseling. If you're in need of information about healthcare coverage or budget counseling, see "Health & Money Interim Options" in the next section of this book.

AFFORDABLE HOUSING HOTLINE
The Connection

(612) 922-9000

Twenty-four hour telephone helpline provides callers with listings for Twin Cities rental properties based on caller's needs. Also provides information about Section 8 and subsidized housing. Properties are not pre-screened. Information is provided by property owners. Free.

ALCOHOLICS ANONYMOUS INTERGROUP

WEST METRO
Calls answered 24 hours.
6300 Walker St., Suite 215
St. Louis Park, MN 55416
(612) 922-0880

EAST METRO
Open weekdays and Sundays.
411 Main Street
St. Paul, MN 55102
(612) 227-5502

STATEWIDE REFERRALS
State and nationwide referrals to meeting locations.
(800) 252-6465

Telephone helpline. Comprehensive referral service with extensive listings for crisis counseling centers, social services, health care. Upon request, makes effort to link callers to free or low-cost services.

CHILD CARE RESOURCE AND REFERRAL LINES
(612) 783-4884—Anoka County
(612) 496-2321—Carver/Scott Counties
(612) 431-7752—Dakota County
(612) 341-2066—Hennepin County
(612) 641-0332—Ramsey County
(612) 430-6488—Washington County

Referral helpline. Conducts customized searches for childcare based on client's criteria. Call for information. Fees may apply.

CHRYSALIS

WALK-IN COUNSELING
550 Rice Street, Suite 104
St. Paul, MN 55105
(612) 222-2823

WALK-IN COUNSELING
2650 Nicollet Ave. So.
Minneapolis, MN 55408
(612) 871-0118

RESOURCE REFERRALS
(612) 871-2603

Volunteer-staffed telephone helpline and walk-in counseling service. Targeted to women, age 18 and up. Referrals to support groups, legal assistance. Free or low-cost.

CRISIS CONNECTION

P.O. Box 14958
Minneapolis, MN 55414
(612) 379-6363

Telephone helpline. Open 24 hours. Crisis counseling, suicide prevention, information and referrals to community resources. Nighttime outreach (team of two counselors meet at client's home or public location for crisis intervention).

FARE SHARE

Ramsey Action Programs

2213 Charles Avenue
St. Paul, MN 55114
(612) 644-9339
(800) 582-4291

Fare Share is part of a worldwide network allowing individuals to exchange two hours of volunteer service, plus $14, for grocery packages containing meat, produce, condiments and dry goods at a 60% savings. Food is distributed monthly at host sites in Minnesota. Registration and payment in advance is required. Call for information about site locations.

FIRST CALL FOR HELP

WEST METRO
Open 24 hours.
404 So. Eighth St.
Minneapolis, MN 55404
(612) 335-5000

EAST METRO
Open 8 a.m.- 8 p.m.
166 E. 4th St., Suite 310
St. Paul, MN 55101
(612) 224-1133

Telephone helpline. Comprehensive referral service with extensive listings for crisis counseling centers, social services, healthcare. Upon request, makes effort to link callers to free or low-cost services.

GAY AND LESBIAN HELPLINE

310 E. 38th St., Suite 204
Minneapolis, MN 55409
(612) 822-8661   (800) 800-0907

Crisis and referral helpline. Open M-F, noon to midnight; Saturdays, 4 p.m. to midnight. Information and referrals, crisis and support counseling. Serving Twin Cities and greater Minnesota.

HAZELDEN INFORMATION CENTER

Box 11, Center City, MN 55012
(800) 257-7800

Telephone helpline. Referrals to local and national treatment programs or self-help meetings for chemical dependency and other addictions. Phones answered daily, 6 a.m. to 10:30 p.m.

HSI CRISIS CLINICS

7066 Stillwater Blvd. No.
Oakdale, MN 55128
24 Hour Crisis Hotline—(612) 777-4455
(612) 777-5222

Twenty-four hour crisis helpline and daytime walk-in crisis counseling, starting at 9 a.m. Year round. Referrals provided as needed.

LOVE LINES CRISIS CENTER

2535 Central Avenue N.E.
Minneapolis, MN 55418
(612) 379-1199
Fax—(612) 782-0916   BBS—(612) 782-8800

Telephone helpline. Free 24-hour crisis service. Also offers in-person counseling on appointment basis. Sponsored by Christian ministry.

MINNESOTA DEPARTMENT OF HUMAN RIGHTS

500 Bremer Tower
7th Place & Minnesota Street
St. Paul, MN 55101
(612) 296-5663   (800) 657-3704

Legal assistance for individuals with employment discrimination claims. Investigation of claims, filing charges, seeking remedies. Reps hold office hours in many Minnesota communities. Call or write for information.

MINNESOTA FOOD SHELF ASSOCIATION

4025 W. Broadway Avenue
Robbinsdale, MN 55422
(612) 536-9180
(800) 782-6372

Referral helpline. Information and referrals to approximately 330 Minnesota food shelves. Call for information.

TEL LAW
Hennepin County Bar Association

(612) 332-2114

Information and referral line. Recorded information provides referrals to free and other legal services statewide. Messages on topics such as employment law, bankruptcy, home ownership, civil law, family law, criminal law, landlord/tenant rights, consumer concerns, juvenile law and tax law. Free.

ALCOHOLICS ANONYMOUS

STATEWIDE REFERRALS

(800) 252-6465

ST. CLOUD AREA

(320) 253-8183

24-hour helpline. For anyone with a desire to stop drinking.

ARROWHEAD ECONOMIC OPPORTUNITY AGENCY

702 Third Ave. So.

Virginia, MN 55792

(218) 749-2912   (800) 662-5711

Referral helpline and social service agency. Serving Aitkin, Carlton, Cook, Itasca, Koochiching, Lake and St. Louis Counties.

BI-COUNTY COMMUNITY ACTION

Bemidji, MN 56601

(800) 332-7161   Fax—(218) 751-8452

Referral helpline. Serving Beltrami and Cass Counties. Assistance with fuel, rent and family services.

BLUE EARTH COUNTY INFORMATION AND REFERRAL

Mankato, MN

(507) 389-8374   Fax—(507) 389-8379

Referral helpline. Open weekdays during business hours. Serving greater Mankato and Blue Earth County.

CARITAS FAMILY SERVICES

Catholic Charities

305 No. Seventh Ave.

St. Cloud, MN 56303

(320) 252-4121   Fax—(320) 252-4508

Crisis intervention and assistance. Provides counseling and short-term assistance. Food shelf, clothing and household items available to individuals or families in financial crisis. Call for appointment. Free.

GREATER MINNESOTA

CONTACT

(507) 451-9100   (800) 648-2330

Crisis and referral helpline. Serving greater Owatonna, Steele and Waseca Counties. Counseling and referrals to social services.

FAMILY RESOURCE CENTER HELPLINE

P.O. Box 500
Chisago City, MN 55013
(612) 257-2400   Fax—(612) 257-4727

Referral helpline. Open business hours. Serving Chisago, Isanti, Kanabec, Mille Lacs and Pine Counties. Referrals to social services, food shelves, housing, legal and debt assistance.

FARE SHARE
Ramsey Action Programs

2213 Charles Avenue
St. Paul, MN 55114
(612) 644-9339   (800) 582-4291

Fare Share is part of a worldwide network allowing individuals to exchange two hours of volunteer service, plus $14, for grocery packages containing meat, produce, condiments and dry goods at a 60% savings. Food is distributed monthly at host sites in Minnesota. Registration and payment in advance is required. Call for information about site locations.

FIRST CALL FOR HELP - GRAND RAPIDS

P.O. Box 113
Grand Rapids, MN 55744
(218) 326-8565   (800) 442-8565—Regional only
(218) 326-4634—TTY

Crisis and referral helpline answered 24 hours. Serving Itasca County. Crisis intervention, active listening and referral.

FIRST CALL FOR HELP
Lake Country Community Resources
P.O. Box 54
Fergus Falls, MN 56538
(218) 736-2856   (800) 257-5463
TDD—(218) 736-3372   Fax—(218) 736-3727

Referral helpline. Open business hours. Serving Becker, Douglas, Grant, Otter Tail, Stevens, Wadena and Wilkin Counties.

FIRST CALL FOR HELP - NORTHFIELD
Northfield Community Action Center
1001 Division
Northfield, MN 55057
(507) 645-9301

Referral helpline. Open business hours. Serving Rice County. Referrals to social services, emergency, food and housing assistance.

FIRST CALL FOR HELP - ST. CLOUD
P.O. Box 542
St. Cloud, MN 56302
(320) 252-3474
(800) 828-5709

Telephone helpline and referral service, answered M-F, 24 hours. Serving Benton, Morrison, Sherburne, Stearns, Todd and Wright Counties. Referrals to crisis counseling and support.

GAY AND LESBIAN HELPLINE
310 E. 38th St., Suite 204
Minneapolis, MN 55409
(612) 822-8661   (800) 800-0907

Open M-F, noon to midnight; Saturdays, 4 p.m. to midnight. Information and referrals, crisis and support counseling. Serving Minnesota.

HAZELDEN INFORMATION CENTER

Box 11, Center City, MN 55012

(800) 257-7800

Referrals to local/national treatment programs, self-help meetings for chemical dependency, other addictions. Answered daily, 6 a.m.-10:30 p.m.

HEARTLAND COMMUNITY ACTION AGENCY

310 So. First Street

Willmar, MN 56201

(320) 235-0850   (800) 992-1710   Fax—(320) 235-7703

Referrals to social services. Open business hours. Serving Kandiyohi, McLeod, Meeker and Renville Counties.

HUMAN DEVELOPMENT CENTER

1401 E. First Street

Duluth, MN 55812

(800) 634-8775   Fax—(218) 728-4404

Crisis and referral helpline serving northeastern Minnesota. Provides 24-hour mental health counseling.

INTER COUNTY COMMUNITY COUNCIL

P.O. Box 189, Oklee, MN 56742

(218) 796-5144   Fax—(218) 796-5175

Calls answered M-F. Serving Clear Water, East Polk, Pennington and Red Lake Counties. Assistance with food, energy and household repairs.

LUTHERAN SOCIAL SERVICES

26 Seventh Avenue No.

St. Cloud, MN 56303

(320) 251-7700

Referral helpline directs callers to agency services including individual and group counseling for families, couples and individuals.

MILLER DWAN MEDICAL CENTER CRISIS LINE
502 E. Second Street
Duluth, MN 55802
(218) 723-0099   (800) 766-8762
Fax—(218) 720-1452

Crisis and referral 24-hour helpline. Serving St. Louis County. Phone assistance, direct referrals to crisis team. No charge for call, initial assessment for crisis team counseling.

MINNESOTA DEPARTMENT OF HUMAN RIGHTS
500 Bremer Tower
7th Place & Minnesota Street
St. Paul, MN 55101
(612) 296-5663   (800) 657-3704

Legal assistance for individuals with employment discrimination claims. Services include investigation of claims, filing charges, seeking remedies. Representatives hold office hours in many Minnesota communities. Call or write for information.

MINNESOTA FOOD SHELF ASSOCIATION
4025 W. Broadway Avenue
Robbinsdale, MN 55422
(612) 536-9180   (800) 782-6372

Referral helpline. Information and referrals to approximately 330 Minnesota food shelves. Call for information.

MINNESOTA VALLEY ACTION COUNCIL
(800) 767-7139   Fax—(507) 345-2414

Referrals to fuel assistance, employment, food, transportation, housing, loans. Open business hours. Serving Blue Earth, Brown, Faribault, Le Sueur, Martin, Nicollet, Sibley, Waseca and Watonwan Counties.

PRAIRIE 5 COMMUNITY ACTION COUNCIL, INC.

7th St. and Washington Ave.
P.O. Box 695
Montevideo, MN 56265
(320) 269-6578   (800) 292-5437   Fax—(320) 269-6570

Referral helpline. Open business hours. Serving Big Stone, Chippewa, Lac qui Parle, Swift and Yellow Medicine Counties. Referrals to social services for fuel assistance, family self-sufficiency programs.

S.E. MINNESOTA INFORMATION AND REFERRAL

1414 Northstar Drive
Zumbrota, MN 55992
(507) 732-8506   (800) 277-8418

Referral helpline. Open business hours. Serving Dodge, Freeborn, Goodhue, Houston, Mower, Olmstead, Rice, Steele and Wabasha Counties. Referrals to community day care and other services.

ST. LOUIS COUNTY SOCIAL SERVICES

Information and Referral
Government Service Center, Room 109
320 W. Second Street
Duluth, MN 55802
(218) 726-2222   (800) 232-1300   Fax—(218) 726-2163

Referral helpline. Open business hours. Serving Lake and St. Louis Counties. Referrals to social services.

SOUTHWEST OPPORTUNITY COUNCIL

515 Tenth Street
Worthington, MN 56187
(800) 658-2444

Referrals to social services, emergency housing, childcare, energy assistance. Answered weekdays. Serving Murray, Nobles, Pipestone and Rock Counties.

THE CRISIS LINE
1321 No. 13th Street
St. Cloud, MN 56303
(320) 253-5555

24-hour crisis helpline. Serving Benton, Sherburne, Stearns, Wright Counties. Handles alcohol, drug or mental health emergencies.

TRI-VALLEY OPPORTUNITY COUNCIL
102 No. Broadway
Crookston, MN 56716
(800) 584-7020   Fax—(218) 281-6681

Referrals to social services, financial counseling, childcare, fuel assistance. Answered weekdays. Serving Marshall, Norman and Polk Counties.

WEST CENTRAL MINNESOTA COMMUNITIES ACTION
307 Eighth Avenue West
Alexandria, MN 56308
(320) 762-3010   (800) 492-4805   Fax—(320) 762-2305

Referrals to community social services. Open business hours. Serving Clay, Douglas, Grant, Pope, Stevens, Traverse and Wilkin Counties.

WESTERN COMMUNITY ACTION
203 W. Main
Marshall, MN 56258
(507) 537-1416   (800) 658-2448

Referrals to social services, transportation, fuel assistance. Open weekdays. Serving Cottonwood, Jackson, Lincoln, Lyon and Redwood Counties.

HEALTH & MONEY

INTERIM OPTIONS

If you're worried about healthcare coverage or household finances because you're unemployed, be reassured that some programs or services may offer solutions.

Most helplines listed in the preceding section make referrals to local community-based services or crisis support. However, on the following pages, we've identified a sampling of direct sources of information about:

♦ Interim Healthcare Options

♦ Credit, Debt and Budget Counseling

Because we know that the costs of healthcare can be a challenge for those in job transition, on the following pages we've tracked down options to explore. If you are a member of a professional association, find out if the national organization offers low-cost group healthcare coverage. For those over age 50, **AARP** (American Association for Retired Persons, page 219) offers several programs that may result in savings to members: mail-order prescriptions and group healthcare insurance.

If you are facing a financial crisis now, budget counselors can help you improve your money management techniques or intervene on your behalf to negotiate a payment plan with creditors.

Take heart. There's help available.

HEALTHCARE OPTIONS

Referral helplines listed in the preceding section can also help you identify affordable or crisis healthcare services.

ASSURED CARE

Hennepin County Community Health Department
(612) 348-6141

For residents of Hennepin County who meet income and other eligibility requirements. Program offers discounts of 25-75% on healthcare services received at Assured Care network clinics based in Hennepin County.

COBRA

Consolidated Omnibus Budget Reconciliation

COBRA is a federal law which allows you, under specific circumstances, to continue to buy group health insurance through your former employer for 18 months up to three years. You may be eligible for COBRA if you are:

◆ Unemployed or if the number of hours you work has been reduced.

◆ An employee who accepted a new job with a new health plan that limits coverage of pre-existing conditions including pregnancy.

◆ A dependent of a deceased worker.

◆ A divorced spouse of an employee.

◆ Losing your status as a "dependent child" under health plan rules

Under this federal law, you're included if you worked for an employer with more than 20 employees on at least 50 percent of the working days in the previous calendar year and who offered health plans. The law doesn't apply to the federal government and certain church-related organizations. COBRA coverage must be identical to that provided to current employees but the employer can charge up to 102 percent of the group premium.

HILL-BURTON FACILITIES

(800) 638-0742

In 1946, Congress passed a law giving some acute-care hospitals and other health facilities money for construction and modernization. In return, these facilities agreed to provide a certain amount of free services to people unable to pay. Hill-Burton facilities provide free care each year but may stop once that a specified volume is reached. Eligibility for services is based on income guidelines. Call for a list of local Hill-Burton facilities.

MINNESOTACARE

444 Lafayette Road No.
St. Paul, MN 55155
(612) 297-3862   (800) 657-3672

MinnesotaCare is a comprehensive family healthcare plan designed for permanent Minnesota residents who are uninsured, ineligible for other medical assistance and meet specific income guidelines. Premiums are based on income and family size. Call for eligibility guidelines and application.

NEIGHBORHOOD HEALTHCARE NETWORK

2550 University Ave. W., Suite 460S
St. Paul, MN 55114
(612) 489-2273

Targeted to medically uninsured, underinsured and underserved individuals. Referrals made to community health centers in Twin Cities metro area that provide medical, dental and mental health services. Eligibility based on income guidelines and family size. Call for information. Sliding fee.

UNIVERSITY OF MINNESOTA DENTAL CLINIC

515 Delaware St. S.E.
Minneapolis, MN 55455
(612) 625-2495

Open to the public with some eligibility guidelines. Offers savings up to 25-35 percent on wide range of dental services. Call for information.

HEALTHCARE HELPLINES

CHILDREN'S HOSPITAL OF ST. PAUL
Children's On Call Health Line
(612) 220-6868
(800) 869-1320

Open to the public. Registered nurse answers questions about child and adolescent behavior and medical problems. No charge.

FAIRVIEW HEALTHWISE
Referral and Resource Line
(612) 672-7272
(800) 824-1953

Open to the public. Provides physician referrals and information about classes and programs at Fairview health systems. No medical advice provided. Calls answered weekdays, 7 a.m. to 9 p.m.

HEALTHEAST TELE-HEALTH LINE
Referral and Health Line
(612) 232-2600

Open to the public. Physician referrals and opportunity to talk to registered nurse for information. No medical advice given. Leave message for return call. No charge.

HEALTHSPAN MEDFORMATION
Referral and Health Line
(612) 863-3333

Open to the public. Provides physician referrals and information on health screenings, classes and programs, as well as taped messages on a variety of health concerns. Also offers the opportunity to talk with registered nurse.

MEDICA'S NURSELINE
Referral and Health Line
(612) 797-4800   (800) 962-9497

For Medica members only. Calls answered 24 hours a day. Registered nurse answers general health-related questions and provides referrals to Medica physicians and facilities.

NATIONAL MENTAL HEALTH ASSOCIATION
Referral and Information Line
(800) 969-6642

Open to the public. Free brochures on over 200 mental health topics. Referrals to local mental health professionals. Calls answered 24 hours.

ST. FRANCIS REGIONAL MEDICAL CENTER
Referral and Health Line
(612) 445-2273

Open to the public. Physician referrals and the opportunity to speak with a registered nurse for health information. Calls answered 24 hours.

ST. PAUL RAMSEY MEDICAL CENTER / RAMSEY CLINIC
Tel-Med Health Line
(612) 221-8686

Open to the public. Recorded information on 29 health-related topics including general health and illness, emergency care, first aid, children's health and illness, drugs and alcohol and more. No charge.

UNIVERSITY OF MINNESOTA HOSPITAL AND CLINIC
Health Line
(612) 626-6000   (800) 688-5252

Open to the public. Calls answered weekdays, 7:30 a.m. to 5 p.m. Opportunity to speak to a registered nurse about general health questions. Physician referrals are also provided to U of M physicians.

CREDIT & DEBT COUNSELING

CARITAS FAMILY SERVICES
305 No. 7th Avenue
St. Cloud, MN 56303
(320) 252-4121   Fax—(320) 252-4508

Financial counseling program. Offers budget counseling, debt repayment planning, seminars. Helps negotiate with creditors. Financial management support group. Free (nominal fee for seminars). Call for appointment.

CONSUMER CREDIT COUNSELING SERVICE
National Referral Line
(800) 388-2227

Voice-messaging system provides locations of Consumer Credit Counseling Service offices including several in the Twin Cities and greater Minnesota. Services may vary by location but generally include budget counseling, debt repayment plans and money control workshops. Sliding fee.

FAMILY & CHILDREN'S SERVICE
414 So. 8th Street
Minneapolis, MN 55404
(612) 339-9101   Fax—(612) 339-9150

Assists with money management and debt repayment plans. Also offers individual and family mental health counseling. Sliding fee.

FAMILY SERVICE INC.
166 Fourth St. E., Suite 200
St. Paul, MN 55101
(612) 222-0311   TDD—(612) 222-0175   Fax—(612) 222-8920

Assessment of financial situation, budgeting, debt repayment plans. Crisis intervention for threat of mortgage foreclosure, eviction, utility shut-offs or harassment by creditors. Money management workshops. Mental health counseling available. Sliding fee.

RELOCATION
RESOURCES

When a job move means packing up the Chevy for a trek to a new town, your stress level can hit a high note. Fortunately, there are many local services that can help you weather the task.

◆ Before you commit to a job-related move, carefully weigh the benefits and trade-offs. Find out about the quality of life in the prospective community. Gather information about the local schools, taxes, housing costs, crime rate, commuting distances, shopping areas, recreational activities and other criteria.

◆ Call a family meeting. Discuss the opportunity to relocate with your spouse or partner and children. How will a move affect them? Don't overlook how a move may affect others you may leave behind: aging parents, friends and relatives.

◆ Figure out the bottom-line costs of the move. Ask a prospective employer to explain relocation benefits that may apply.

◆ Internet resources can quickly help you gather information about local real estate, newspapers, moving companies, maps, community profiles and more. Here are a few to explore:

Relocation-Net: http://users.mwci.net/~relonet/

Minnesota Network Navigator: http://www.mndex.com/MNDEX/

CityNet: http://www.city.net/countries/united_states/

CityLink: http://www.NeoSoft.com:80/citylink/

AFFORDABLE HOUSING HOTLINE

The Connection

(612) 922-9000

Listings for Twin Cities rental properties based on caller's needs. Information about Section 8, subsidized housing. Properties are not pre-screened. Free.

APARTMENT SEARCH

2756 Hennepin Ave. So.
Minneapolis, MN 55408
(612) 870-0525   (800) 832-7476   Fax—(612) 870-0619

Free apartment locater service with computerized database of Twin Cities rentals. Call for information.

BURNET RELOCATION MANAGEMENT

Burnet Realty

7550 France Ave. So.
Edina, MN 55435
(612) 844-6500   (800) 388-8700   Fax—(612) 844-6515
E-mail: brmrelo@visi.com

Real estate agency. Offers free housing and other information about Minnesota communities. Resources describe local attractions, schools, maps, taxes and include community profiles. Call for information.

CHILD CARE RESOURCE AND REFERRAL LINES

(612) 783-4884—Anoka County
(612) 496-2321—Carver/Scott Counties
(612) 431-7752—Dakota County
(612) 341-2066—Hennepin County
(612) 641-0332—Ramsey County
(612) 430-6488—Washington County

Referral helpline. Conducts customized searches for childcare based on client's criteria. Call for information. Fees may apply.

EDINA REALTY RELOCATION SERVICES

1400 So. Highway 100, Suite 200
Minneapolis, MN 55416
(612) 591-6400   (800) 328-4344   Fax—(612) 545-7709

Real estate agency. Provides extensive free relocation packet with information on Twin Cities housing, community profiles, shopping, maps, attractions, schools, taxes, major employers, search firms. Also provides rental assistance and computerized information comparing departure city with destination city for affordability of housing. Call for information.

ENROLLMENT OPTIONS HOTLINE

Minnesota Department of Children, Families & Learning
(612) 296-1261   (800) 657-3990   Fax—(612) 296-5846

Information about how to approach the process of selecting a school in Minnesota. Also provides referrals to publications to help assess Twin Cities and greater Minnesota school districts and alternative educational programs, both public and private.

GREATER MINNEAPOLIS CHAMBER OF COMMERCE

81 So. 9th Street, Suite 200
Minneapolis, MN 55402-3223
(612) 370-9111—Information Order Line

Provides publications to newcomers on housing, schools, income taxes, parks and recreation, community profiles and more. Career Kit provides regional job-search resources and other helpful publications. Call or write for ordering information and fees.

LIVING GUIDE

8030 Old Cedar Avenue, Suite 214
Bloomington, MN 55425
(612) 858-8960   Fax—(612) 858-8923

Free guide to Twin Cities and St. Cloud rental properties. Published three times a year. Call or write for information.

METROPOLITAN COUNCIL DATA CENTER

230 E. Fifth Street
St. Paul, MN 55101
(612) 291-8140   Fax—(612) 291-6464

Extensive information about the greater metropolitan area with census data, maps, housing reports and economic profiles. Call or write to receive publications directory. Publications sold at modest fees.

MINNESOTA CHAMBER OF COMMERCE

30 East 7th Street, Suite 1700
St. Paul, MN 55101
(612) 292-4650   (800) 821-2230   Fax—(612) 292-4656

Upon request, many Chambers of Commerce provide a relocation packet that includes local community information. To locate a particular Minnesota Chamber, contact the organization above.

RELOCATING IN THE TWIN CITIES

Star Tribune Merchandise
425 Portland Avenue
Minneapolis, MN 55488
(612) 673-9005   Fax—(612) 673-7894

Sourcebook published by Star Tribune offers profiles of neighborhoods and communities along with information about property taxes, crime statistics, schools, shopping, attractions, plus local telephone, gas, electric and cable companies. Call for information. $5.95 plus shipping.

SAINT PAUL AREA CHAMBER OF COMMERCE

332 Minnesota, Suite 200
St. Paul, MN 55101
(612) 223-5000

Provides relocation publications to newcomers with information on schools, local government, hospitals, taxes, crime statistics, community profiles, major employers, rental information and more. Call for pricing.

STAR TRIBUNE FAX SERVICE

(612) 525-3555

The Star Tribune daily Twin Cities newspaper provides reprints of past Homes section articles by fax at a fee. Article topics cover choosing a neighborhood and deciding whether to rent or buy. Call for recorded ordering instructions. Touch-tone phone required.

STAR TRIBUNE FONAHOME

6228 Bury Drive
Eden Prairie, MN 55346-1718
(612) 673-8888   (800) 362-4663

Free relocation service provides information on Minnesota housing, day care, schools, local attractions, trailing spouse assistance and more. Free rental housing information and videotapes about properties in the greater metro area. Also offers referrals to out-of-state relocation resources. Call for information.

TWIN CITIES TOURISM INFORMATION LINE

Greater Minneapolis Chamber of Commerce

(612) 370-9103

Recorded message describes Twin Cities attractions, lodging, restaurants, shopping, current events, sporting events and transportation.

CHAPTER SIX

FOR
HOT TIPS &
SMART IDEAS

S o you claim you're the perfect job seeker. Your resume's so slick you could snare an interview at the White House. You can recite your work skills and accomplishments—in Spanish and English. Your career goals are clearly articulated in a 40-page personal marketing plan. You've memorized every employer in the Yellow Pages.

And that's not all. Every day, you scan the classifieds, call job hotlines and cruise the Internet for work opportunities. You've networked at every pancake breakfast from Mora to Mankato. By now, every recruiter in town knows your name—and probably your shoe size.

So why isn't it working?

Perhaps it's time for some smart tips and common-sense solutions from the experts.

On the following pages, the editors of the *Minnesota Job Seeker's Sourcebook* have compiled dozens of great ideas to spruce up your work search and survive transition.

Sometimes "success" is in the details.

LOST YOUR JOB? TIME TO ACT!

APPLY FOR REEMPLOYMENT INSURANCE.

If you've lost your job through no fault of your own, you may be eligible for reemployment insurance. Apply immediately. Unemployed persons receive weekly payments up to 26 weeks with occasional extensions. The size of the check and number of payments depend on past employment and wages prior to losing your job. Apply at the nearest Job Service/Reemployment Insurance office. See locations starting on page 19.

If you're entitled to reemployment insurance, use it. Don't let your pride get in the way. This interim income will soften the financial blow of losing your job and allow you to put efforts into job seeking.

SECOND TIME AROUND?

If you've been laid off before, even multiple times, don't panic. You probably mastered basic job-search techniques during earlier transitions and learned from past mistakes. Immediately tap the networking contacts who were most effective in the past. Try not to despair or let discouragement drag you down. At the same time, consider how you can improve your job-keeping skills. If you're over 50, take a good look at your computer proficiency. There's no avoiding the need for these skills in today's workplace. Don't put it off. Sign up for a short-term class through an adult education program.

FIND INSURANCE COVERAGE.

Try to maintain healthcare insurance during this stressful time. COBRA is a federal law which allows you, under certain circumstances, to continue to buy group healthcare coverage from your former employer for up to 18 months. For interim healthcare options, see page 250.

CUT YOUR EXPENSES—NOW.

Make an accounting of your household financial standing. Add up your income, including any severance pay you've received, then deduct your expenses. Look for short-term spending cuts. Try to reduce spending on restaurant meals, dry cleaning, cable TV, long-distance telephone calls, house cleaning help, newspaper and magazine subscriptions or health club memberships. You may benefit from budget counseling to keep your household on track. See page 255.

BE PREPARED FOR AN EMOTIONAL ROLLER COASTER.

Job transition is one of life's major stressors. Expect to feel a gamut of emotions like shock, disbelief, anger, depression, sadness—even periods of elation. A job support group can help you and your family members accept your situation and move forward. Financial crisis can further strain an already difficult time. Seek professional help, if needed. See listings for transition support services starting on page 221.

THINK ABOUT INTERIM EMPLOYMENT.

Strapped? No severance? Don't let mounting debt add to your stress. Consider freelance, contract or temporary employment as an interim source of income while you're hunting for your first-choice job. A temp job can also keep you active in the workplace and expand your networking contacts. If you're receiving reemployment benefits, check with a Job Service/Reemployment representative about whether a temporary job will have an effect on your benefits.

CONSIDER YOUR OPTIONS.

A job loss or other transition motivates some folks to re-think their direction. Now may be the time to go back to school for a quick class or advanced degree. Maybe you want to start a business. Relocate in a community with brighter job prospects. Or examine the benefits of early retirement. For helpful resources, see listings starting on page 189.

SLOW DOWN. GET FOCUSED.

◆ It's up to you to take charge of your own career strategy. You can no longer expect an employer to be responsible for your training and development or provide you with a guaranteed job. In today's changing workplace, your best safety net is your own initiative.

◆ Focus on your selling points. The more you know about what you have to offer, the less time you'll spend in a hunt. Here's a technique to try: Imagine you're a product on a department store shelf. Who would want to buy you? What unique benefits do you offer? Why *shouldn't* a customer pass you by in favor of the competition? How can you improve your packaging or content? Use your answers to create a clear resume and to interview with confidence.

◆ If you have access to the Internet or commercial online service, some Web sites offer online self-assessment exercises that can help you clarify your strengths, personality, interests and values resulting in a better job fit. Also available are software packages for job seekers offering step-by-step guidance through the self-assessment process. See listings for online and multimedia resources beginning on page 97.

RESUME WARM-UPS

◆ Most resumes focus on job titles and responsibilities. Stand out by focusing on your accomplishments. Employers want some indications of how you can add value to their organizations.

◆ A chronological resume lists employment by dates and shows your progression of responsibilities. Most hiring professionals prefer this style. It gives them a clear picture of your career path and emphasizes your latest positions. If you have solid experience in your field, use this style.

◆ Thinking about fudging on the facts on your resume? Think again. Today, many employers use fact-checking services that quickly and easily confirm employment dates, academic degrees and other information.

◆ When you develop your resume, keep in mind that you're saying to an employer: "Ask me more about this skill or accomplishment." Be prepared to elaborate on every resume detail during an interview.

◆ Many hiring decision-makers don't like slick resumes. Stick to the basics. Keep it simple. The upper two-thirds of the page is considered the "hot spot." Information listed here is the most likely to be read.

◆ Learn how to produce a scannable version of your resume. Many employers now use computers to pre-screen applicants by scanning their resumes for keywords. These words are generally the qualifications that match those required for the job: specific job titles, skills, education, industries, occupational level, length of employment and others. Phrases such as, "Achieved sales goals in competitive market," that work on paper are largely ignored by the computer.

Check your local library or bookstore for guides that explain how to prepare a scannable resume that gets results. A few tips: Avoid formatting with fancy fonts, boldface, italics, underlining, lines, shading and boxes.

◆ If you're 50 or over, don't get screened out for being too old, too expensive or over-qualified. Avoid phrases like: "I have over 25 years of data processing experience." This information could date you. Instead, use descriptions like *seasoned professional* or *senior clerk.*

◆ Are you interested in more than one type of job? Develop multiple resume versions, each stressing different aspects of your accomplishments.

◆ For additional resume tips, see page 65.

THE INTERVIEW

◆ Do your homework before an interview. Thoroughly research information about an employer. Few applicants take the time and your research will get noticed. At the very least, employers expect you to know who they are and what they do. Scan local newspapers for news about the organization's business expansions, new products, acquisitions or promotions. Discussing recent company news during the interview can make a positive impression. For resources useful in researching employers, see listings beginning on page 98 and 119.

◆ If you suspect that you're the first to interview for a job, try to re-schedule. The last person interviewed has a better chance of being hired than the first. If you're offered a choice of Tuesday, Wednesday or Thursday, take Thursday. The worst day to interview is Monday. The worst time to interview is late afternoon.

◆ When given the choice, schedule interviews between 9:30-11 a.m. or 1:30-3:30 p.m. During these times, you won't have to share the spotlight with distractions such as lunch or the end of the business day.

◆ It's the job of the human resource department to screen you out, not screen you in. Typically, an HR rep has three concerns: Are you qualified? Will you fit in with the company? Is the compensation a match? You'll improve your chances of getting noticed if you find a way to connect directly to the hiring manager.

◆ During an interview, make eye contact, especially when making an important point. Employers are more likely to hire candidates who look them directly in the eye. Some interviewers believe that they can read an applicant's personality, confidence, honesty and sincerity in their eyes.

◆ Leave little to chance when preparing for an interview. Anticipate commonly asked questions and practice your responses. Write down questions in advance to ask about the job or the company. Bring extra copies of your resume, references and letters of recommendation. Complete the job application in advance. Have pens and notepaper handy.

◆ Arrive ten minutes early to scope out the work environment. How are visitors and workers dressed? Is the atmosphere formal or casual? Quick-paced and noisy? Cool and reserved? Thumb through some company brochures. This quick investigation can help you feel more prepared during the interview.

◆ For over-50 job seekers: It's illegal for prospective employers to ask your age, so most won't. During an interview, focus on your career achievements, not on your grandchildren. Avoid statements like: "I may be older than most of your employees, but..." Invest in an updated wardrobe. During the interview find ways to share examples about how you have kept abreast of technological changes.

◆ Once you get past the initial screening with a human resources representative, your next step is to meet with a manager or group who will actually make the hiring decision. Be prepared for multiple interviews with several individuals including managers and prospective teammates—a process that could take several weeks. And don't expect a lightening-quick job offer either. Employers are extremely cautious about making a costly hiring mistake.

◆ If you want the job, express your interest in joining the organization's team. Close the interview with a summary of your background and the key reasons you feel you're a good fit for the job. Ask about your next step. Is there another interview? Should you call back? By when? Then follow through.

ETIQUETTE, IMAGE & FOLLOWUP

◆ Studies indicate that many hiring decisions are made in the first few minutes of an interview. Your clothing, tone of voice, body language, energy level, handshake and early non-job-related conversation may have more impact than you think. Everything about you, from the condition of your shoes to how you greet the receptionist, contributes to crucial first impressions.

◆ Buy the best suit or dress you can afford for interviewing, even one that's a step above the quality you normally wear. This investment could reduce your job-seeking efforts by one week or more.

◆ Don't run the risk of offending employers with overpowering cologne or after-shave. To be safe, avoid using any scented products.

◆ Send thank-you notes!

◆ Followup calls are essential after you've sent your resume. Call the employer one day after you think your resume was received. Never wait more than four days. A followup call will ensure your resume doesn't get buried, and may increase your chances of winning an interview.

◆ Set high standards when you communicate. Every form of correspondence is a reflection on the quality of your work. Proofread for misspellings, poor grammar and typing errors. Each time you finish a cover letter, read it out loud. If you stumble or run out of breath, you need to do more editing.

◆ Use your tape recorder to improve your communication skills. Record a conversation with a friend. Play the tape back and listen closely. Are you speaking too quickly? Using too many 'ums' or run-on sentences? Are you overusing jargon or certain expressions?

NETWORK AND STAY CONNECTED

◆ Don't keep your job hunt a secret. Most jobs come from networking. Make a list of everyone you know. Neighbors. Former classmates. Old buddies. Past co-workers. Church members. Sorority sisters. Ask contacts for leads to anyone they know who has an opportunity or contact in your field. Follow up on all referrals. Keep in touch with contacts every four to six weeks or they may assume you've landed a job.

◆ Don't ask your contacts for a job. Instead, ask them to open doors for you. Try questions such as: "Can you help me set up a meeting with...?" or "Would you help me find a contact at XYZ company?"

◆ During a networking meeting: 1) Tell about yourself, your goals, your background; 2) Find out about the individual's company or industry; 3) Ask for help with additional networking contacts or leads.

◆ Ask contacts to critique your resume to be sure they understand your background—crucial for any future referrals they may make.

◆ Here's an easy way to keep your contacts interested in helping you. Prepare a folder for each contact. Jot down notes about the individual's interests, hobbies, family and occupation. When you come across a news article or tidbit that might interest them, add it to their folder. Send clippings to them regularly with a friendly note.

◆ When scheduling a networking meeting, ask for a short 15-minute meeting at times like 9:15 or 9:45 instead of 9:00 or 10:00. This reassures busy people that your meeting will be brief.

◆ Consider using a one-page newsletter to stay in touch with your networking contacts. Keep it brief, bright and informative, with status reports and requests for additional contacts or industry information.

JUST FOR COLLEGE GRADS

OUR THANKS TO COLLEEN KAY WATSON, PRESIDENT, CAREER PROFESSIONALS, INC., AND PAST PRESIDENT, MINNESOTA ASSOCIATION OF PERSONNEL SERVICES, WHO CONTRIBUTED MANY OF THESE TIPS.

◆ Avoid sending out aimless resume mailings or responding to misleading ads. Most of the tips found on the preceding pages apply to you too. *Focus and prepare for your job hunt.*

◆ It's no surprise that networking is your best bet in landing your first job. Talk with your parents, relatives and family friends about who they know who is working in your field. Then muster up the courage—or apply the discipline—to ask for a brief meeting.

◆ Your chances of landing a job improve if you completed an internship or have career-related experience, according to a survey by Michigan State University. The survey also notes that grads who are in demand show initiative, drive and enthusiasm, are quick learners, independent thinkers, computer savvy and sensitive to multiple cultures.

◆ Temporary agencies may help you get useful work experience without a long-term commitment. A temp job can give you an insider's look at the workplace and a chance to acclimate to its daily routine. Another plus: a surprisingly high number of temps are subsequently hired. To locate temp firms, see listings starting on page 145.

◆ Don't overlook the obvious. Explore services at your college career office. Services may include job postings, resume help, job-search coaching and more. For a listing of college career centers in Minnesota, see page 77. If you have access to the Internet, most colleges maintain Web sites that may provide online career support to graduates. Minnesota colleges and Internet addresses can be found beginning on page 201.

◆ See if your college career office offers an alumni mentorship program that connects you to seasoned alums in your field. These professionals may be able to help you expand your network or track down job leads. Ask one or more to review your resume or make suggestions about the work experience you need to move forward.

◆ Don't despair if your college is located out of state. The career office may still be able to help you. Inquire about online services and mentorship programs described in the preceding paragraphs.

◆ If you own a computer, an alumni perk to look into is free or low-cost access to the Internet. Part hype, part astounding potential, a cyberspace job search may be a worthwhile effort. See page 98.

◆ If you want a recruiter's help, don't turn to search firms; they work only with experienced personnel. Employment agencies may be helpful but some charge fees. If fee-based services are not for you, ask a reputable employment firm to show you only employer-paid fee positions.

◆ Even if you have a suitcase full of impressive degrees, don't hit the job market with inflated expectations of immediate responsibilities or income. Positions open to college grads are generally entry-level. That means, part-grunt work, part-learning experience. Keep in mind that a career is NOT a ladder; it's a series of building blocks that get moved and re-assembled throughout your worklife. As you add skills and experience, you add another block to the stack. Your genuine interest in learning, patience and positive attitude will pay off.

◆ Seventy percent of recent college grads leave their first employer within 18 months. This may not reflect well on your resume. Once you land a job, try to stay with your employer *at least* two years. Remember—the workplace operates on a different schedule from your college routine which presented new challenges every 3-4 months.

QUICK & PAINLESS $$ CUTBACKS

Money Saving Tips During Times of Transition

◆ Review your insurance policies. Consider raising the deductible on your auto insurance policies. Ask your agent for quotes on combined auto and homeowners policies. Inquire about discounts for non-smokers, non-drinkers, good students and accident-free drivers.

◆ Scour your closets, workroom, garage and junk drawers for new, unused items—wiper blades, spray paint, photo refill pages, clothing, etc. Return them to the store where purchased for cash or credit. Many stores accept returns (even on purchases made eons ago) without a receipt, as long as the store name appears on the price sticker.

◆ Plan dining-out excursions around coupons and special deals. Early-bird dinners can save you money if you're willing to eat during off-peak hours or on slower days of the week.

◆ If a computer purchase is critical to your job transition, check into discounted prices on demos, one-of-a-kind units or discontinued models at your local electronics store. Some retailers specialize in selling previously-owned computers and may offer discounts of 25-50%.

◆ Your junk may be someone's treasure. Look through collections of records, baseball cards, military clothing, sports equipment, collectibles, antiques and old books. Collectors and second-hand stores may pay for your items. Before parting with valuable items, have them appraised.

◆ Treat yourself to a beauty makeover. To promote their products, department stores offer makeovers with free cosmetics or perfume samples. Resist the urge to purchase now. As your cash flow improves, you can return the favor.

◆ Store coupons can make an astounding difference in your grocery bill. Check Sunday circulars. If you find a particularly valuable coupon on an item you use, ask friends or relatives to save their circulars for you.

◆ Check your workshop, basement and garage for metal scraps and wire. Quick extra cash awaits you from your local recycler.

◆ Weigh the costs and benefits of your current checking and savings accounts. Your financial institution may allow you to switch to a reduced or no-fee account at no charge. Order your next batch of checks through the companies that advertise them in the Sunday circulars. You may save up to 50%.

◆ Family fun: Most museums, zoos and art galleries sponsor free-admission days; some roller-skating rinks, bowling alleys and community swimming pools may offer off-hour pricing. Don't forget about $1 movie theaters or renting videos and CDs at the public library.

◆ For more low-cost family fun, contact the Minnesota Office of Tourism (612) 296-5029 or (800) 657-3700, for a recorded listing of statewide events and festivals. Many offer free attractions.

◆ Meeting your networking contacts at restaurants can cost a bundle. To cut costs, schedule meetings over breakfast or mid-morning coffee rather than dinner. You may save $3-7 per meeting.

◆ Set a weekly cash budget and stick to it. Avoid using ATMs or credit cards to advance yourself cash. Make casinos off-limits.

◆ Students at local training schools need to practice their new skills, so many training centers offer a variety of student-provided services to the public at incredible savings. Enjoy a gourmet meal, receive a facial or massage, have your car repaired, get a haircut— even have dental work done, all at deeply discounted prices.

◆ Don't deprive yourself of the chance to attend professional conferences and meetings. Some organizations let potential members attend a few events before joining. Others offer reduced or deferred fees to unemployed members. Still others permit a few individuals to attend conferences in exchange for working on site for part of the day.

◆ Consignment and thrift stores are full of surprises. Update your wardrobe with high-quality, gently worn clothing. You may even find new items donated at the end of the season by major retailers.

◆ The federal government publishes a variety of consumer resources including: **"Solving Credit Problems"** (#350C, 50¢), **"Managing Your Debts: How to Regain Financial Health"** (#348C, 50¢), **"66 Ways to Save Money"** (#352C, 50¢). Mail your request and payment to: Consumer Information Center, P.O. Box 100, Pueblo CO 81002. You can also read these publications and others for free online: http://www.gsa.gov/cgi-bin/imagemap/cicmap?365,189

◆ Cultural events are not necessarily taboo just because you're on a budget. Call local theaters and ask if you can volunteer as an usher or in some other capacity for free admission to the current production. Don't forget about rush seats and student or alumni discounts.

◆ Supermarket and other grand openings can be cheap family fun and a chance to take advantage of special one-time discounts, give-aways and free food.

◆ During summer months, the Farmer's Market and roadside stands offer bargain prices on a variety of produce. The day trip can also be an inexpensive weekend activity.

◆ If you're a homeowner, don't let excess funds remain idle in your escrow account. The month after your lender pays your property taxes, contact Customer Service to request a refund for any overpayment.

INDEX OF RESOURCE LISTINGS

◆ ◆ ◆

ORDER FORM

Did you borrow this book?

Here's how to order your copy of the *Minnesota Job Seeker's Sourcebook.*

"BEST INFORMATION GUIDE"
MINNESOTA BOOK AWARD

Telephone orders: TWIN CITIES **(612) 545-5980** NON-METRO **(800) 555-9058**
Please have VISA or MasterCard handy.

Postal orders: Mail a copy of this order form with payment to:
Resource Publishing Group Inc.
P.O. Box 573, Hopkins, MN 55343

☐ Please enter my order for _____ copies of the
Minnesota Job Seeker's Sourcebook at **$21.95** each.

NAME_____

ORGANIZATION_____

ADDRESS_____

CITY _____ STATE_____ ZIP_____

PHONE (_____) _____

SHIPPING & HANDLING:

Add $4.50 for the first book; $1.00 for each additional book.

SALES TAX:

Add 6.5% sales tax for books shipped to a Minnesota address.
Exempt from sales tax? Please attach a copy of your exemption certificate.

PAYMENT:

☐ Check: Amount enclosed $ _____

☐ Credit Card: ☐ VISA ☐ MasterCard

CARD NUMBER _____

NAME ON CARD _____ EXP. DATE _____

SIGNATURE_____